GOGMAGOG

GOGMAGOG

The Buried Gods

by

T. C. LETHBRIDGE

Routledge and Kegan Paul

LONDON

First published 1957
© *by Routledge and Kegan Paul Ltd.*
Broadway House, Carter Lane, E.C.4.
Printed in Great Britain by
Western Printing Services Limited, Bristol.

Queene and Huntresse, *chaste, and faire,*
Now the Sunne *is laid to sleepe,*
Seated in thy silver chaire,
State in wonted manner keepe:
    HESPERUS intreats thy light,
    Goddesse, excellently bright.

Earth, let not thy envious shade
Dare it selfe to interpose;
CYNTHIAS shining orbe was made
Heaven to cheere, when day did close:
    Blesse us then with wished sight,
    Goddesse, excellently bright,

Lay thy bow of pearle apart,
And thy cristall-shining quiver;
Give unto the flying hart
Space to breathe, how short soever:
    Thou that mak'st a day of night,
    Goddesse, excellently bright.

BEN JONSON [1573–1637]

v

Acknowledgements

I am most grateful to the Cambridge Preservation Society for allowing me to defile their hill-side with excavations. Although many of them did not believe in the existence of the figures, they never attempted to throw me down the slope. The work was carried out, like many other important investigations in the last fifty years, by the voluntary members of the Cambridge Antiquarian Society and is no concern of the Department of Archaeology.

My wife has been an indefatigable assistant in helping with measurements, wheeling barrows, typing out the manuscript and correcting proofs. No one could have done more.

Mr. C. F. Tebbutt was also a great help, not only in the actual digging, but in supervising volunteers. So also was Mr. S. Hopkin, who not only worked himself, but brought trained toolmen over with him.

I have also had much kind encouragement from Sir Cyril and Lady Fox, Sir Thomas Kendrick, Dr. Margaret Murray and Mr. Harold Bayley. Their immediate grasp of the character and meaning of the work was a great pleasure. From them one learns to realize the great gulf which separates those who really use their brains to solve important questions and those who think that anything can be answered if you dig a big enough hole.

Contents

List of Figures

Plates

Chapter One

THE story really begins with a fairy tale. I am fond of fairy tales and regret that the teller of this one should have been such an unpleasing character. In fact, to judge from his biography in the learned article on his life written by the late H. W. C. Davies for the *Encyclopaedia Britannica*, he must have been a thoroughly beastly person. A Clerk in Holy Orders, who could boast that he had borne false witness against a girl who had spurned his amorous advances and succeeded in getting her burnt for heresy, deserves the title of beastly if anyone does.

Gervase of Tilbury, this teller of fairy tales, was a kinsman and school friend of Patrick, Earl of Salisbury, and later employed by Henry, the heir to the throne of England. On the death of Henry in A.D. 1183, Gervase was thrown on his own resources and wandered about Europe trying to ingratiate himself at the courts of various ruling princes. About A.D. 1211 he had managed to worm his way into the friendship of the Emperor Otto IV, and wrote a book for his pleasure entitled, *Otai Imperialia*. In this hotch-potch of political theory, history, geography and folk-lore, occurs the fairy story, which I now quote in full from the translation of the late Arthur Gray, Master of Jesus College, Cambridge, which was printed in the 1911 volume of the *Proceedings of the Cambridge Antiquarian Society*:

'In England, at the boundary of the diocese of Ely, there is a town named Cantabrica, in the neighbourhood of which there is a place called Wandlebiria, from the fact that the Wandali when ravaging Britain and savagely murdering the Christians, placed their camp there. Now, where they pitched their tents on

the hill-top, there is a level space surrounded with entrench-
ments and with a single entrance, like a gate. There is a very
ancient tradition, attested by popular report, that if a warrior
enters this level space at the dead of night, when the moon is
shining, and cries, "Knight to knight, come forth", immediately
he will be confronted by a warrior, armed for fight, who,
charging horse to horse, either dismounts his adversary or is
dismounted. But I should state that the warrior must enter the
enclosure alone, though his companions may look on from outside. As a proof of the truth of this I quote a story told to me by
the country people of the neighbourhood. There was in Greater
Britain, not many years ago, a knight redoubtable in arms and
possessed of every noble quality, among the barons second in
power to few, to none in worth. His name was Osbert, son of
Hugh. One day he came as a guest to the town I have mentioned,
and, it being winter time, after supper, as is the fashion with
great folk, he was sitting in the evening by the fireside in the
family of his wealthy host, and listening to the tales of exploits
of ancient days; and while he gave ear to them it chanced that
one of the people of the country mentioned the wondrous legend
aforesaid. The brave man resolved to make personal trial of the
truth of what he was told. So he selected one of his noble
squires, and, attended by him, went to the place. In complete
armour he came to the appointed spot, mounted his steed, and
dismissing his attendant, entered the camp alone. He cried aloud
to discover his opponent, and in response a knight, or what
looked like a knight, came forth to meet him, similarly armed,
as it seemed. Well, with shields advanced and levelled lances
they charged, and each horseman sustained his opponent's shock.
But Osbert parried the spear thrust of his antagonist, and with
a powerful blow, struck him to the ground. He was on his feet
again in an instant, and, seeing that Osbert was leading off his
horse by the bridle, as the spoils of conquest, he poised his lance
and hurling it like a javelin, with violent effort he pierced
Osbert's thigh. Our knight however in the exultation of his
victory, either did not feel or did not regard the wound, and his
adversary having disappeared, he came out of the camp vic-
torious, and gave the horse which he had won to his squire. It
was tall, active and beautiful to behold. He was met on his
return by a number of the family, who marvelled at the tale,

2

were delighted at the overthrow of the knight, and loudly applauded the bravery of this illustrious baron. When Osbert took off his arms and discarded his iron greaves he saw one of them was filled with clotted blood. The family were amazed at the wound, but the knight scorned fear. The neighbours, aroused from slumber, came thronging together, and their growing marvel induced them to keep watch. As evidence of the victory the horse was kept still tethered. It was displayed to public view with its fierce eyes, erect neck and black mane; its knightly saddle and all its trappings were likewise black. At cockcrow the horse, prancing, snorting and pawing the earth, suddenly burst the reins that held it and regained its native liberty. It fled, vanished, and none could trace it. And our noble knight had a perpetual reminder of the wound which he had sustained, in that each year, as the same night returned, the wound, though apparently cured and closed, opened again. So it came about that that famous warrior, some years later, went over sea, and, after performing many deeds of valour against the heathen, by God's will ended his days.'

The story is, of course, elaborated by Gervase, but it has the appearance of being a genuine piece of traditional folk-lore, dating from before the time that he left England. It is probably safe to say that the story was current in the Cambridge Area as early as A.D. 1177 and possibly long before that.

Now, fairy stories are of two kinds; they are either entirely imaginary; or they may be traditional, handed down for many generations and embroidered by some teller of tales. Gervase expressly states that this particular story is an old tradition. I hope to show, as this book goes on, that not only was Gervase's tradition genuine, but that it was founded on remarkably solid fact.

Stripping off the Medieval husk of Gervase's embroidery, the tradition appears to be this:

There was some mysterious warrior, who could be seen in the moonlight, near the entrance to the earthwork, which is now known as Wandlebury. He was probably connected in some way with one, or perhaps two, other figures and a supernatural horse.

At this stage the warrior is not of abnormal size; he is only uncanny. When we meet him next he has become a giant and his horse, his opponent and the squire have disappeared. In fact, he has ceased to be a figure of mystery and is an entirely concrete picture, which the scholars of Cambridge went to see.

I first published this account in *The Times* (12 June 1936) at the end of a long correspondence on the question of the origin of the name 'Gogmagog Hills'. This letter was quoted in Morris Marples' book, *White Horses and Other Hill Figures*; but, since it was my letter, I shall quote it again, for it introduces both the earliest and the latest written accounts we have of a Giant on these hills:

'To the Editor of *The Times*.
'Sir,

Gog Magog Hills.

'Gogmagog, or Gourmaillon, was undoubtedly responsible for the name of these hills. His figure cut in the downland turf, either inside Wandlebury Camp itself or on the hillside close beside it, was still visible in the middle of the eighteenth century, as the following extract from the manuscripts of William Cole, the antiquary, shows:— "In a quaint book by Bishop Hall in 8vo., printed by Edward Blount and William Barrett, called the Discovery of a New World or a Description of the South Indies, with this running title, The description of Tenter-Belly, and subscribed the Cambridge Pilgrim, at p. 44, is this:—

' "A Giant called All Paunch, who was of an incredible Height of Body, not like him whose Picture the Schollers of Cambridge goe to see at Hogmagog Hills, but rather like him that ought the two Apple Teeth which were digged out of a well in Cambridge, that were little less than a man's head." When I was a boy, about 1724, I remember my Father or Mother, as it happened I went with one or other of them to Cambridge, the road from Baberham there lying through the Camp (now blocked up by the house and gardens inclosed in it of my Lord Godolphin), always used to stop and show me and my Brother and Sisters the figure of the giant carved on the Turf; concerning whom there were then many traditions now worn away. What became of the two said teeth I never heard.

'It is probable that Gogmagog was to be seen in the camp itself, for a tradition, published some years ago by the Master of Jesus in the *Proceedings of the Cambridge Antiquarian Society*,

4

tells us that if we go to the entrance of the camp in the moonlight and cry, "Knight to knight come forth", a giant will
emerge and fight with us. It is possible that the Elizabethan
edict which forbade students to attend festivities at Wandlebury
is not unconnected with the survival of fertility rites performed
at this figure. It is curious that a similar figure also existed at
Oxford. I have been unable to trace the slightest sign of our
Gogmagog either on the ground or from the air.'

As it happens, Bishop Joseph Hall, under the name Mercurius
Britannicus, had originally published his book in Latin, at
Frankfurt in A.D. 1605. William Cole was quoting from a
translation, published in English by J. Healey about A.D. 1609.
The original Latin version ran: 'Vastae molis, parem non illi,
cujus effigiem nostrates Acedemici e vicino colle excisam invisunt
et admirantur.' There is no mention of Hogmagog or Gogmagog. The picture is simply described as 'cut out of a neighbouring hill'.

John Layer, a Cambridge Antiquary, some of whose works
were published by the Cambridge Antiquarian Society in 1935,
wrote about A.D. 1640. He remarked: 'I could never learn how
these hills came to be called Gogmagog Hills, unless it were
from a high and mighty portraiture of a giant wch the schollars
of Cambridge cut upon the turf or superficies of earth within
the said trench, and not unlikely might call it Gogmagog, which
I have seen but it is now of late discontinued.'

This is all very well. Anyone might think that here was
valuable first-hand evidence. As it happens, it is incorrect in its
two main statements. The giant was not within the 'said trench';
neither did the scholars cut it, although they may have scoured
it. It is very hard to see how Layer, who went about the country
collecting antiquarian material, could have got this wrong. I
suppose there is a possibility that the scholars may have tried
their hand at cutting a giant on their own, but it cannot have
been the giant which was well known in Cambridgeshire up to
about a hundred years ago. This giant was said to be on the
slope of a hill visible from the village of Sawston, some two and
a half miles to the south-west of Wandlebury. Two independent
persons witnessed to this.

The first of these was Mr. Samuel Cowels. 'Sammy' spent

most of his working life in the University Museum of Archaeology and Ethnology at Cambridge. Here he sat, year in and year
out, on a high stool to which somebody had fastened the back
of an old wooden chair. Hunched over a bench, this little gnome-
like figure took infinite pains in making up broken pottery or
cleaning and mounting bronzes. Sammy was very versatile.
On one occasion the curator, Baron Anatole von Hugel dreamt
that broken pots could be restored with pieces of cork. Next
day he asked Sammy whether he could use this apparently in-
tractable material. (This was before the days of the universal
use of Plaster of Paris for such work.) Sammy said that he
thought he could. Several pots still remain in the Museum as
witness of Sammy's skill; with handles, faces and other ornaments all beautifully carved to replace the missing portions.

On another day a smashed Roman glass jar, something like a
square-faced gin bottle with a handle, was taken down to Sammy
with a cremation burial inside it and he was asked to stick the
glass together. Some days later someone remarked, 'Sammy is
being a long time mending that glass jar.' We went down to see
what was happening. There was the glass jar finished, but
Sammy was very busy over something else. He was just ending
the sticking together of an entirely unknown glass vessel. This
was a little funnel-shaped thing of colourless glass, wound
round with a thin spiral coil of opaque yellow. It was as thin as
a watch glass and had been smashed into hundreds of tiny
pieces. 'Where did you get that, Sammy?' he was asked. 'I
found it among them cremated bones,' he replied.

But all Sammy's work was not of this nature. Once an appal-
ling stench began to penetrate the upper floors of the Museum.
People hurried down the stairs to find out the cause of this
terrible pollution. Sammy was in the gas cupboard of the work-
room, but the door was open. He was bending over a large tank
filled with bubbling blackish liquid in which were grinning
several human skulls. He was, in fact, boiling the old dry flesh
off some heads from New Guinea to prepare them for the Physical Anthropologists. 'Oh! Sammy! How can you stand this?'
cried the onlookers. 'I likes them gruesome jobs,' was Sammy's
reply.

I first got to know Sammy in 1925. At intervals through the
years, he used to ask, 'When are you going to look for that

Giant?' (I was excavator for the Cambridge Antiquarian Society.) His story of the giant was this: As a child he had known an old man who told him that, when he was a child, the giant could be seen from Sawston. This gave me a rough estimate of perhaps a hundred years since the giant had been seen. Precisely the same information had been given to Mr. M. C. Burkitt, the archaeologist, by Mr. Guy Maynard, who at that time was Curator of the Saffron Walden Museum. Old men had told Maynard that the giant used to be visible from Sawston. Tales of the giant appear to have circulated for at least twenty miles around Cambridge. In all cases, however, it seems to have vanished about a hundred years ago.

Other traditions circulated also, which appear to have some relation to the hills and these have come under my personal notice. People, who were children in Cherry Hinton some fifty years ago, were not allowed to play in the chalk-pit on the slope of the hill above the village because Gog and Magog were buried there. Cherry Hinton is two miles north of Wandlebury. A second tradition, which is widespread in the district, concerns a buried golden chariot. When I first heard this story, about twenty-five years ago, the chariot was said to be buried in the Fleam Dyke near Mutlow Hill.

Mutlow Hill, three miles east of Wandlebury, is a remarkable place. The hill itself is a Bronze Age barrow, which was dug by the Hon. R. C. Neville about a hundred years ago. In it were, amongst other things, glass beads brought to Britain from the eastern Mediterranean in the fifteenth century before the Birth of Christ. The barrow, which was presumably the site of a moot in Saxon times, seems to have been used as a sighting point for the construction of the Fleam Dyke. This great linear earthwork, barring the Icknield Way, was excavated by Sir Cyril Fox in 1922–3, and shown to belong to the close of the Roman period or to Saxon times. A circular Roman building, either a temple, or possibly a signal station, stood close to Mutlow Hill. The interest in the place is not, however, confined to the construction of these monuments, it is concerned with what happened near them.

The Icknield Way was the great through route in prehistoric times, from the chalk downs of the south-west, over the Thames, along the slopes of the Chilterns and so up into Norfolk near

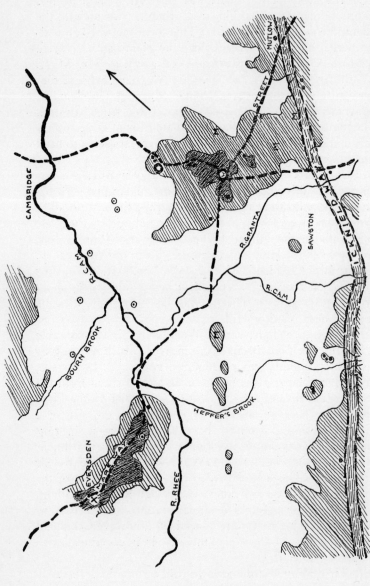

Fig. 1—Sketch-map of Wandlebury Area. (Width approximately twelve miles.) Large Circles show Pre Belgic forts W indicating Wandlebury. Dots mark barrows. Ringed dots Iron Age Settlements, etc. Dotted lines show suggested Iron Age routes. Land over 100 ft. light shading. Land over 200 ft.

the mouth of the Wash. It may never have been canalized into a metalled road; but consisted of a series of numerous trackways, perhaps forming a belt of a quarter of a mile wide. All along its course are the old camping places and the burial mounds of Bronze Age men and women, who probably moved along it in seasonal migrations, driving their flocks and herds before them. The Mutlow Hill was just one barrow out of hundreds, few of which can now be seen except from the air. At Mutlow Hill, however, another ancient road crossed the Icknield Way and was known in Saxon times as the 'Street'.

When the land is ploughed and the light is right, you can see numerous dark lines on the soil, all converging on Mutlow Hill. These are the old hollow ways of the Icknield Way and the Street. At the point where they meet the Fleam Dyke, the vallum of the earthwork has been 'slighted' in ancient times. Part of it has been thrown back into the ditch. But the hollow ways pass both under and over the slighted bank. Here in more recent times the iron bosses of Anglo-Saxon shields have been found and here the rabbits turned up human bones.

I sometimes wonder whether the tramps, who often camp among the trees and bushes which cover the dyke, pass restful nights or whether they suddenly wake to some nameless horror. They could hardly be expected to know that those white things, lying among the rabbit scratchings beneath the bushes, are the bones of men slain in war. Yet this is what they must be. Here some forgotten action was fought and the victors ordered the bank to be thrown back so that they might pass freely over it in future. Part of it was used to cover their dead.

Now, during the last few years, I talked to a woman who had been a child in one of the houses near Mutlow Hill. I asked her whether she knew where the golden chariot was buried in the dyke. She replied that she had always heard that it was not in the dyke itself, but in the road which passed the dyke and went on to West Wratting and the south-east. This road, however, is the Street. Its two hollows, which pass over the levelled dyke beside the human bones, head westward in the direction of Wandlebury and can be picked out most of the way, either on the ground or from the air.

The people living on the estate of Wandlebury apparently believed that the chariot was buried on the hill itself. I did not get this last piece of information till after I had been working for some time on the hill; but I have no reason to think that it is not genuine.

I have written down these details because they have some bearing on the value of folk tales in general. Here we have traditions of the burial of two giants and of a golden chariot. The location of the burials varies, but it must be remembered that the stories were all told to children. 'Along that road, which passes over the dyke up there, a golden chariot was buried.' 'You must not play in that clunch pit or the giants, Gog and Magog, who were buried long ago, may come after you.' The parents may have known the exact place where the giants, or the chariot, were buried and not bothered to explain this to children who were not able to appreciate the topography of the neighbourhood.

These are all the traditions I have met concerning the Gogmagog Hills. Before taking the matter any further, it seems a good plan to investigate this Gogmagog. He is not mentioned in Gervase. He does not seem to appear till the seventeenth century. The name may not have been applied in Elizabethan times. This does not really seem probable, for there are no less than four Megg's or Mag's Hills within a radius of three and a half miles of Wandlebury, and I know of no others in the district. It looks as if the name Mag or Megg was of old association round about. It also suggests that Gog was a later addition and that the original personage was Magog. This is pure guesswork, but it may be worth while to remember it while taking the question a little further.

Gog and Magog, of course, occur in the Bible (Ezekiel, Chapter XXXVIII). 'Son of Man, set thy face against Gog, the land of Magog, the chief prince of Meshech and Tubal, and prophesy against him. And say, Thus saith the Lord God; Behold I am against thee, O Gog, the chief prince of Meshech and Tubal; And I will turn thee back, and put hooks into thy jaws, and I will bring thee forth, and all thine army, horses and horsemen, all of them clothed with all sorts of armour, even a great company with bucklers and shields, all of them handling swords: Persia, Ethiopia and Libya with them; all of them with shield and Helmet; Gomer, and all his bands; the house of Togarmah of the north quarters, and all his bands: and many people with thee.'

In Elizabethan days and for many years to come, the Bible was almost the entire reading matter for most people in England. Here is a description of Gog, armed for war and apparently about to invade Palestine. But Magog is a land and not an individual.

The first writer, who seems to speak of Gogmagog as one person, was apparently Geoffrey of Monmouth, who wrote a book entitled *Historia Britonum*. He died in A.D. 1154. This history is a remarkable work. For long after his death it was regarded as truthful history. Then opinions changed and it was denounced as complete fable, or at best as something so embroidered as to be disregarded.

Geoffrey certainly took whole sections out of the works of older historical writers. He expanded them and put them into the garb of his own day. He claimed to have a copy of an ancient Welsh book from which he drew other information. It seems certain that he had such a book. There are details in the history of the civil war at the time of Allectus (A.D.297), which are not found elsewhere and which make perfectly good sense when removed from their medieval embroidery. He knew, as many archaeologists have noted, that stones were brought to Stonehenge from overseas; a fact which has only been proved in recent times by an investigation of the petrological composition of the stones. It seems very hard, however, to explain his story of the settlement of Britain by people of Trojan descent, but for one possibility. These people of Trojan ancestry, he said, came to Britain starting from Italy. There were Veneti at the head of the Adriatic. There were also Veneti in Amorica, which later became Brittany.

The leader of the Trojan immigrants, called Brutus, had a general called Corineus to whom he entrusted Cornwall. It is on the borders of Cornwall that the incident occurs in which Gogmagog is involved and it is in Brittany that the only other Gogmagog, Gourmailhon, is found.

There is some tradition here, recorded by Geoffrey in such a way that it is almost incomprehensible. But it does not seem as if it were a product of his imagination. Here is the story of Gogmagog as translated in the Bohn's edition of Geoffrey's History:

'The island was then called Albion, and was inhabited by none but a few giants. Notwithstanding this, the pleasant situation of the places, the plenty of rivers abounding with fish, and the engaging prospect of its woods, made Brutus and his company very desirous to fix their habitation in it. They therefore passed through all the provinces, forced the giants to fly into the caves of the mountains, and divided the country among them according to the directions of their commander. After this they began to till the ground and build houses, so that in a little time the country looked like a place that had been long inhabited. At last Brutus called the island after his own name, Britain, and his companions Britons; for by these means he desired to perpetuate the memory of his name. From whence afterwards the language of the nation, which at first bore the name of Trojan, or rough Greek, was called British. But Corineus, in imitation of his leader, called that part of the island which fell to his share, Corinea, and his people Corineans, after his name; and though he had his choice of the provinces before all the rest, yet he preferred this country, which is now called in Latin Cornubia, either from its being in the shape of a horn (in Latin Cornu), or from the corruption of the said name. For it was a diversion to him to encounter the said giants, which were in greater numbers there than in all the other provinces that fell to the share of his companions. Among the rest was one detestable monster, named Goëmagot, in stature twelve cubits, and of such prodigious strength that at one shake he pulled up an oak as if it had been a hazel wand. On a certain day, when Brutus was holding a solemn festival to the gods, in the port where they at first landed, this giant with twenty more of his companions came in upon the Britons, among whom he made a dreadful slaughter. But the Britons at last assembling together in a body, put them to the rout, and killed them every one but Goëmagot. Brutus had given orders to have him preserved alive, out of a desire to see a combat between him and Corineus, who took a great pleasure in such encounters. Corineus, overjoyed at this, prepared himself, and throwing aside his arms, challenged him to wrestle with him. At the beginning of the encounter, Corineus and the giant, standing, front to front, held each other strongly in their arms, and panted aloud for breath; but Goëmagot presently grasping Corineus with all his might, broke three of his

12

ribs, two on his right side and one on his left. At which Corineus, highly enraged, roused up his whole strength, and snatching him upon his shoulders, ran with him, as fast as the weight would allow him, to the next shore, and there getting upon the top of a high rock, hurled down the savage monster into the sea; where falling on the sides of craggy rocks, he was torn to pieces, and coloured the waves with his blood. The place where he fell, taking its name from the giant's fall, is called Lam Goëmagot, that is, Goëmagot's Leap, to this day.'

Now it is a well-known fact that there used to be one, or more, giants on Plymouth Hoe. One was certainly known as Gogmagog in A.D. 1486. Two figures are mentioned bearing clubs in A.D. 1602. The whole story can be found in Marples' *White Horses and other Hill Figures*. Whether there was only one giant in the first place and a second was added in the sixteenth century and called Corineus after Geoffrey's hero is of no immediate importance to our investigation. The fact remains that there was a giant figure of Gogmagog at Plymouth in the reign of Henry VII, and a tradition relating to a similar giant was recorded by Geoffrey three hundred years before. The situation is comparable with the tale told by Gervase of Tilbury and the prosaic reports of Hall, Layer and Cole regarding our Gogmagog Hills. It is curious, however, that if Gervase had heard the name Gogmagog mentioned in connection with our hills, he did not use it. He must have been familiar with Geoffrey's History, for it was one of the most popular works of the day and he was, in some sort, an historian himself. It does not seem as if he can ever have heard the name in this connection.

Arthur Gray, in his paper about the Wandlebury legend, produced another interesting piece of information. Quoting from M. Sebillot's *Traditions de la Haute Bretagne*, he connects Gogmagog with the Gourmailhon of a haunted earthwork near Goven in the department of Ile de Vilaine. The circular earthwork, known as the Butte, or Tombeau de Gourmailhon, was supposed to contain hidden treasure, but any treasure seeker was confronted by a supernatural goat. Knowing what we do of the other two cases, it is tempting to regard this supernatural goat in the light of a lingering tradition of some other horned figure; something of this world and not of some other.

13

The other celebrated Gog and Magog figures are those of the two giants of the London Guildhall. Twice destroyed by fire and twice renewed, these figures are known to have been in existence in the time of Henry V. It is believed, however, that they were not always known as Gog and Magog. Giant images were formerly popular in many places in western Europe. They still survive as Carnival figures in the south of France and in Spain. Others were known in the Low Countries. Judging by the manner in which representations of saints are carried in processions in the Latin countries, it seems most probable that these carnival figures had once another significance and perhaps may be compared with the Hindu gods also carried in procession. Be that as it may, the Guildhall figures appear to have changed their names to Gog and Magog and some people believe that one of the figures was once female. Others prefer to think that they should be Gogmagog and Corineus. There is no clear evidence as to who they were. At the moment the only original Gogmagog we can point to in Britain is the first of the missing figures on Plymouth Hoe. Attempts ought to be made to look for him. He sounds remarkably like the great 'Hercules' figure at Cerne Abbas in Dorset.

But who or what was Gogmagog? Was he one person or two? Was the Goëmagot of Geoffrey the same as Gogmagog? Mr. Harold Bayley in his *Archaic England* makes very reasonable suggestions in answer to some of these questions. He believes Gog to have been a great pagan deity and Magog a Mother Goddess. Goggle is 'gog euil' or gog eyed; giggle is the same. A whole gamut of words follow suit and may bring in their train the 'shiela-na-gig', now used as a technical term for obscene female carvings on churches. Much of this appears very sound reasoning. One thing, however, may not perhaps fit. It is reasonable to see a relationship between all these words, Gogmagog and Gog and Magog. It is not quite so easy to see how Geoffrey's Goëmagot became Gogmagog, without assuming a spelling mistake in the original manuscript.

Goëmagot appears to be much closer to the Breton Gourmailhon than it does to Gogmagog. It is hard to understand how gour or goe could ever change to Gog, as it seems to have done in the three centuries between A.D. 1154 and 1486, without deliberate interference from outside. Was Gogmagog a Biblical twist given to an ancient Celtic name which sounded vaguely like it? If this is correct, then there were no Gogmagog figures at all until the end of the Middle Ages, when Bible reading became general. A gogmagog was simply an obviously pagan figure; preferably with rolling eyes. Goggle, giggle, ogle and the rest followed in its train. Gog was the King of Evil in the Bible and what could be more natural than to apply the word to effigies which were clearly non-Christian. Perhaps the term survives today in the child's grotesque 'Gollywog', a word which I have heard applied to a shiela-na-gig by no less a person than that famous anthropologist, the late Dr. A. C. Haddon. He, when bored by the discourse of the incumbent on the architecture of a church near Wisbech, remarked to me, 'Come outside, Tom, and let's see if we can find any gollywogs on it.' Unfortunately we were unable to please him by finding one.

The neighbourhood of Wisbech is incidentally celebrated for the grave in its vicinity of the hero, or giant, Hiccathrift or Hiccafrith. This warrior, who fought a battle with a wheel for a buckler and an axle-tree for a sword, seems to me to have been 'The trust of the Hiccas' or 'Iceni', and was probably a Celtic god. His grave was formerly pointed out and a stone, known as his candlestick, preserved in a Marshland Church.

I have wandered somewhat from the problem of Gogmagog. The point I wish to make is that we have yet to show whether the name is of very great antiquity. The London figures were not known at first as Gog and Magog. The Cambridge Gogmagog may have had no known name at all in the Middle Ages. The Plymouth figure had a name something like Gogmagog; but which was possibly a different one. Gogmagog, like Gollywog, may then have been a term for a type and not for a specific figure. It came into use perhaps, as the result of the general reading of the Bible, at the close of the Middle Ages, to describe any large pagan effigy. This idea may be quite wrong, but we must be cautious before we assume that the Gogmagog Hills were always called by that name. The processional 'Hob Nob' of Salisbury may well belong to the same family.

If this is the correct interpretation, anyone in Elizabethan England might have spoken of the Long Man of Wilmington, or of the Cerne Giant, as a Gogmagog; although the name of the Cerne Giant was almost certainly 'Helith'. One of the

15

entries in the Plymouth audit book specifically mentions 'the' Gogmagog, as if it were one of several and not unique. '1566–7. 20d. New cutting the Gogmagog.' (Marples after R. N. Worth.)

It is not possible to say at this stage whether Gogmagog was the ancient name for the figure on the Gogmagog Hills or not. On the whole, the evidence tends to suggest that it was given to the figure by the members of the University at a relatively late period and that it stuck because no one remembered the original. It is only by chance that the name of the Cerne giant was preserved in a medieval account. No trace of it appears to have remained in the neighbourhood, unless the place name authorities are at fault. They maintain (*Place Names of Dorset*) that names in the vicinity of the Cerne giant, which are compounded with 'hell', Hell Wood, Hell Corner, Ellston have nothing to do with the name 'Helith' by which he is supposed to have been designated in the thirteenth century (Walter of Coventry. See Flinders Petrie: *The Hill Figures of England*). They say that 'hell' only refers to a dark and shady place. They may be right; but I seem to remember that Hell Tor, on the edge of Dartmoor, was always associated with a giant, who threw rocks, including Hell Tor and Blackingstone Rocks at another, as was their wont. It was presumably the other giant who was supposed to have been laid to rest in the Megalithic 'Giant's Grave' on neighbouring Mardon!

Professor Stuart Piggott has given convincing reasons (*Antiquity*, vol. XII) for equating the name 'Helith' with that of Hercules and I feel myself that Hell Tor, at any rate, had a similar origin. 'Hell' names certainly cluster in the neighbourhood of Cerne; just as the 'Megg's' and 'Mag's' hills surround Wandlebury. These hills must not be forgotten. 'Mag' sounds remarkably like a contraction of Magog.

I will return to the Cerne giant later on. For the present I will leave the question of the name Gogmagog undecided. It may be of great antiquity or it may not.

Giant stories are widespread in Britain, but are more common the further you get to the west.[1] This does not mean that the Anglo-Saxons had no giants: Teutonic folk-lore is full of them. It only means that the east of England is not a country where people tend to laze about in a mild climate and tell stories

---

[1] See Dr. M. A. Murray, *Folklore*, 1955.

to while away the time. I have already mentioned two giants in the east and there are doubtless many others.

The west, and in particular the Celtic-speaking lands, is full of giants. I have been taken out by a crofter near Boisdale, in South Uist, to look at the footprints of a giant. One was on a boulder on the slope of a little hill; the other was on a stone many yards away, which formed part of a causeway in a loch, linking up a small island. The first footprint was perfectly clear. It had probably begun as a weathering in the stone and been improved by human agency. The second was not so clear. The first was eighteen inches long and just like the print of a very long foot. The crofter undoubtedly believed that these prints had been made by a striding giant, for had not several of his sheep been killed by lightning when standing near one of them! All giants are not of this character. Some of them are due to the misunderstanding of two languages. Many of our giant stories probably refer to genuine human heroes; but the English speakers have misunderstood a Celtic word.

I had a personal experience of this. In 1950 I was at anchor in the harbour of South Rona, which must be surely one of the most beautiful in the world. Before the Hitler war, the house was occupied by a family who used to keep a light in the window to show benighted fishermen the bearing for their run in. The house is a ruin now and the place deserted, at any rate it was like that in 1952.

Whilst we lay at anchor, my old friend John M. Robertson, who was then a very old man, remarked that there was something on the island which I ought to see. As his gnarled old hands were busy on a splice, he tried to remember what it was. At last it came back to him. It was 'the Giant's cave'. He had not seen it himself. It was somewhere on the opposite side of the island and it was very remarkable. Then I too remembered that some years before a friend had come to me in Cambridge with a story about a pagan temple he had seen on South Rona.

It took my wife and myself a long time to find the cave, for the east side of the island is much broken up by gullies and the heather was long. It turned out to be one of a series of old sea caves on a raised beach, at the foot of what had once been a small headland. The roof was formed by a great arch of contorted rock and the entrance was masked by falls of stone. Inside it presented a remarkable appearance. Large stones had been arranged in neat rows like the seats in a lecture theatre. At the mouth, a great block appeared to have been roughly trimmed into a cube; while in front of the rows of seats, a ring of stones had been formed to catch a drip from the roof in a kind of basin. It was quite eerie to find such a place on a deserted island, with only the passing Stornoway mail boat to remind one that we were living in the present century. The place indeed suggested some kind of religious gathering; but when and for what purpose it had been made and used seemed impossible to guess.

As it happened, there was no difficulty in obtaining some idea of its date. The stone seats were arranged on a hard layer of humus and sheep's dung, perhaps six inches thick. The rain had, however, washed away the outer edge of this and an extensive midden layer was exposed beneath it. This layer presumably represented the giant's rubbish heap. Red deer, sheep, pigs, seals, fishes and shell-fish, including oysters, had been cut up and opened with metal knives. A few small pieces of broken pottery were to be seen. This pottery was apparently of about the fifteenth century of our era. It was not prehistoric. It did not look as if our giant was of any very great antiquity.

A suspicion crossed my mind. When we were back aboard the ship, I asked Old John what the name of the cave was in Gaelic. 'Uamh na gaisgeach,' he replied. Now the usual name for a giant is not 'gaisgeach' but 'fomor'. Gaisgeach means a soldier or hero. So this was not the Giant's cave, but might perhaps be termed 'the cave of the famous warrior'.

I was not able to try to identify this warrior till I was back in Cambridge in the world of books. Far removed from Rona and its hidden sanctuary, I ran to earth what are probably traces of our supposed giant. The first reference comes from *A Description of the Western Isles of Scotland by Mr. Donald Monro, quho travelled through maney of them in Anno 1549*. Donald Monro, elsewhere describes himself as 'Sir Donald Monro, Heighe Deane of the Isles'. Under 'Ronay', he says:

'At the north end of Raasay be halfe myle of sea fra it layes ane Ile callit Ronay mair than a myle in lengthe full of wood and heddir with ane havin for hieland galeys in the middis of it, and the same havein is quyed for fostering of theives, ruggars, and reivars, till a nail upone the peilling and spulzeing of poure pepil. This Ile perteins of McGilly Challan of Rarsay by force, and to the Bishope of the Iles be heritage.'

Of Rarsay (now written Raasay) he says: 'It is excellent for fishing, pertaining to McGylly Challen of Raarsay be the sword; and to the Bishope of the Iles by Heritage. This same McGilly Challan suld obey McCloyd of the Lewis.'

McGilly Challan, a MacLeod of Lewis, therefore took both islands by force and Rona harbour was used as a base for pirates, ready to jump on any ship passing up or down the Inner Channel to the Kyle of Loch Alsh. McGilly Challan, or MacGillychallum, as his descendants came to call themselves, left an evil name which became a saying in the Highlands: 'As bad as MacGilly-challum.' It seems most probable that the pirate galleys were his and that it was his look-outs who occupied the cave and spied from the hill above it, upon the passing shipping. On Raasay he, or his successor, built the little pirate stronghold of Brochel, which figures in one of William Daniell's celebrated prints. Skene (1577–95) in the *Discription of the Isles*, says that Macleod of Raasay 'hes ane strange little castell in this Ile, biggit on the heid of ane heich craig, and is callit Prokill'. By his day then there was no more talk of ownership by the Bishop of the Isles. MacGillychallum's descendants were firmly established.

It seems to me reasonable to conclude that MacGillychallum was the hero, or warrior or giant, from whom the cave took its name.

Further investigations showed that the cave had been used as a Protestant chapel in the latter part of the nineteenth century and that people came from long distances to attend services there. 'She is not so long dead,' I was told, 'the woman that was last christened in it.'

This giant then has only become a giant through the mis-translation of a word from one language to another. If the place name had been put on the map as a translation, it is quite prob-able that MacGillychallum might have become a real giant of folk-lore. This kind of accident has probably happened many times in places where Celtic languages were giving way to English. A giant in a place name need never have existed. The Fomor people themselves started as warlike merchants, who came to Ireland and also Scotland by sea. They ended up as giants, with several rows of teeth.

Some such misunderstanding might well have accounted for Geoffrey's story of Goëmagot; were it not for the fact that a genuine picture of a giant existed on Plymouth Hoe. As it is, however, the probability is that the picture of the giant was far older than the story. This is certainly the case with our Cambridge giant and with the tales which centre around Cerne and the Long Man of Wilmington. The giants were there on the hillsides long before monks and monasteries came into existence. As this book progresses, I hope to be able to show how such a story came into being.

We know reasonably well that no real race of giants ever existed. Abnormally large human beings are occasionally born, but they are 'sports'. If so, all stories about giants, in the past, must be to some extent distortions of the truth. The association, however, of a story of a giant with some particular place is probably correct. If we learn that a particular giant was to be found in some definite place, then either a MacGillychallum or a monstrous effigy probably had some connection with the spot. There may never have been very many effigies. Geoffrey says that when the Trojans came to Britain, 'The island was then called Albion, and was inhabited by none but a few giants.' There must, on the other hand, have been innumerable outlaws, living in caves and such places, to whom the term 'giant' came to be applied. Until the present age, few tales of giants, fairies, trolls, demons and the like, were without some foundation in fact.

Some no doubt were due to purely natural phenomena, like the giant's footprints, which I have mentioned on South Uist. The Gruagach, that grim giantess who appears on a misty hillside and lures personable young men to their doom, could be no more than the well-known Brocken Spectre. However she was also a goddess, with cup-marked stones named after her. I have seen the Gruagach only once. This was in 1921 when climbing the southern hills of Jan Mayen with Mr. J. M. Wordie, the explorer. A gleam of sun through the mist threw the monstrous images of our dirty and unshaven figures on to the fog across a valley. Anyone who did not know how the Brocken Spectre was formed would surely have taken them for giants. Stories of giants in the mountains often must have begun like this. In certain spots they would be seen more frequently than others. I can think of several places where the name of the Gruagach is attached to lonely lochs, or to ruined forts. One sees small ones, of course, often enough when going out of a lighted doorway on a foggy night. To primitive people such figures probably become ghosts.

When, however, all outlaws, Brocken spectres, natural footprints and the rest are removed, there still remain many tales of giants which need further investigation. Here as often as not a missing hill-figure may well lie beneath the turf.

Chapter Two

IN the autumn of 1954, I had the opportunity of looking for Sammy Cowles' giant. Many people had expressed an opinion that it was quite impossible to locate a hill-figure which had once become completely obscured. In most cases they are probably right. To find such a figure it seems necessary to have a hard subsoil free from rain-water gullies, fissures or other natural hollows, and yet a subsoil which would be subject to disintegration by frost and rain when the turf had been removed from it for hundreds of years. I knew that our local chalk, 'clunch' as it is always called, was of this kind; for I have done much excavation work on it. In most places it is perfectly hard, smooth and without fissures; but it quickly dissolves into sludge when exposed to frost and rain.

When working on the local chalk, I frequently use a stainless steel bar to sound through the topsoil for missing ditches or graves. This is no new method. It used to be the normal way of finding and plotting the course of missing, or choked, field-drains. It is much less trouble than trenching for them, but it has some disadvantages. You must use a fairly heavy bar, or it will not do the work. You must use it yourself, for the man in charge of an excavation has to be certain of what lies beneath the soil and cannot trust the report of a subordinate in this matter. My bar is of stainless steel, $\frac{5}{8}$ in. thick and graduated in feet. It is 5 ft. 9 in. long and I fancy it weighs about 14 lb. Unless your hands are reasonably hard, it does not take very long to raise blisters like hen's eggs on them. By then I am wet through and tired. I have great faith in my bar and am quite immune to the knowing glances of those who have not the muscles to wield it. So it seemed that, in spite of the opinions of the 'Dismal Jims', there was a good chance of success if I could locate the right hillside.

Readers will have been able to judge for themselves the clues that were available. The modern opinions of people like Sammy Cowles appeared to rule out all the relatively suitable slopes between Wandlebury and Cambridge. John Layer's account might have been correct; in which case there was little hope that the giant could ever be found, for the level space described by Gervase, immediately inside the entrance to the earthwork, was completely covered by buildings. I therefore went to examine the southern slopes facing Sawston as Sammy had described. These cannot now be seen from the Cambridge road to Linton, for a broad belt of beech trees has been planted there for perhaps a little less than a hundred years. I was pleased to find that not more than two hundred yards of hillside seemed to fulfil the necessary conditions.

The trenches, which now outline the Cerne giant, are about two feet deep from the surface of the ground. The actual chalk rock away from the trenches is probably less than a foot beneath the surface. The outlines are thus about a foot deeper than they were when the turf was first taken off, nearly two thousand years ago, to form the outlines. This is due to two causes. First the action of rain and frost powdered the exposed surface of the chalk and reduced it to paste. Some of this was, no doubt, washed down the outlines of the giant during rain storms. Some, when dry, blew away as dust in strong winds. Then, in course of time, grass began to grow in the hollows.

It was this growth of grass which made it necessary for all hill-figures to be scoured every now and then. The scouring seems to have been connected always with some kind of festivities, which it is reasonable to suppose were survivals of actual religious ceremonies of pagan times. At the Uffington White Horse, these ceremonies took place once in seven years, accompanied by horse races, a fair and beer drinking. At Cerne they took place on the first of May and a Maypole was set up in a little rectangular earthwork above the giant's head.

It is interesting to note that an Elizabethan edict of the Senate of Cambridge University forbade its members to attend festivities held at Wandlebury, for it seems certain that these must have been connected with the scouring of the giant.

On my preliminary investigation of the site, I noted a low mound of made-up soil, containing small lumps of chalk, on the end of the small spur projecting southwards from Wandlebury and forming the slope which faces Sawston. I thought it probable that this mound was the result of tipping the scourings there over a long period of time.

Since it was evident that the giant was no new feature and had probably been in existence for at least seven hundred years, I felt that it was certain that its outlines must have been scraped and weathered considerably below the normal surface of the chalk rock. Soundings with the bar showed that this surface was normally never more than a foot beneath the grass and was often from six to nine inches only. Therefore I felt that if the bar penetrated some inches more than this, I was probably hitting some artificial hollow in the chalk. By putting sticks on the edges of all such hollows, it seemed probable that they might form some recognizable pattern when their positions were measured in and plotted on paper. The process was to be exactly similar to sounding the bottom of the sea with a lead line and making a chart from the positions of these soundings. I had taken part in such an operation in the Carey Islands, in Baffin Bay in 1937, where it was thought advisable to make a rapid survey of the islands and to chart the anchorages for the benefit of future visitors. This had been a very rough affair, but it was the same idea.

It was thought that a series of horizontal soundings across the face of the hillside, at about nine-inch intervals, could hardly fail to hit the giant if he happened to be there. It was, of course, quite uncertain whether he were there or not.

In the course of the first hour's work, I covered about seventy yards of slope and had put sticks in five soft patches. I was rather depressed, because very early in the proceedings the bar recorded a depth of about eighteen inches for a large number of soundings. It seemed that the chalk rock might be less even than I had hoped. Two other places, however, gave recordings of eighteen inches, for only about two feet in each case, with depths of only nine inches for some distance on either side. I felt very hopeful that these might be portions of an outline of the Cerne type. I decided to disregard the long stretch of deep soundings, which I had made first, and to concentrate on the last two. It was fortunate that I did so. Had the first hollow area been examined at once, it is possible that the full secret of the hill might never have been discovered. Without knowing it, I had actually hit off two giant figures in the first hour's work. Never, in the course of my archaeological experience, had a small piece of deduction and a very little field work produced such remarkable results. If work had been concentrated on the first hollow place, it is most unlikely that I ever should have thought of looking for a second giant. All recent accounts for the last three hundred years had only mentioned one. Only in the legend of Gervase of Tilbury was there any suggestion that there might be more.

My wife and I went home that first afternoon knowing that there were indeed soft places on the hillside; but neither of us had the very slightest idea of what was to follow. I am quite certain that no one could have guessed that we should still be busy sounding that hillside sixteen months later. From first to last, the progress of the work was entirely unpredictable.

Having chosen the two hopeful soft spots, the best method seemed to be to follow up possible lines with short lengths of soundings in order to see what form the hollows would take. We had not appreciated what an enormous number of sticks would be needed even for the first figure. The nearest available source of supply was old dry artichoke sticks cut into three-foot lengths. Before long the ground was dotted with hundreds of artichoke stalks, which gave it a most unusual appearance.

At the end of each day's work, the positions of these sticks were triangulated in and recorded in my note book. When I got home and into dry clothes, they were at once plotted on paper. At the end of a week, a definite shape began to form on the paper; but it was utterly incomprehensible. It looked like the rough outline of the head of a man in a bowler hat, with a long tassel hanging from the back of the brim. It was like no giant ever thought of. Long poring over pictures of Iron Age, Bronze Age and even Roman Art, from all over western Europe gave no appreciable help. The only things vaguely resembling my bowler-hatted man were some figures of warriors in pot-like helmets from Certosa in Italy.

At this stage I sent a tracing (Fig. 2) to my friend, Sir Thomas Kendrick, at the British Museum, saying that I had found an impossible figure of a man in a bowler hat and what on earth was it? The reply came back at once on a postcard: 'Rear quarters of an animal. Walking (not galloping) white horse. May the Lord be with you.' Sir Thomas is, of course, amazingly good at all kinds of art forms; but this was a most effective piece of identification.

I sat for a long time looking at my chart and decided that if it indeed represented the rear quarters of a white horse, then there was almost certainly the rear quarters of a human figure

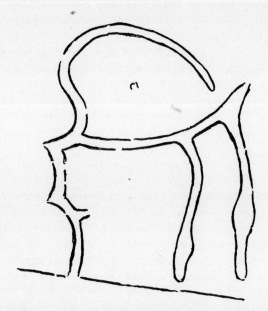

Fig. 2—Earliest version of first figure. This is forty feet high. It was at first suspected of being a male head.

there also. I would leave my outlines and run out another line horizontally to see if I could hit the front side of the body. This was immediately rewarded by the location of another line curving down the hillside.

A tracing of the figure, as it then stood, was sent to Sir Cyril and Lady Fox at Exeter. Sir Cyril has always been the most enthusiastic admirer of Celtic art and as author of the *Archaeology of the Cambridge Region*, was well fitted to give an opinion. Back came a telegram: 'Female with two horses probably Epona congratulations.' This was most encouraging, but

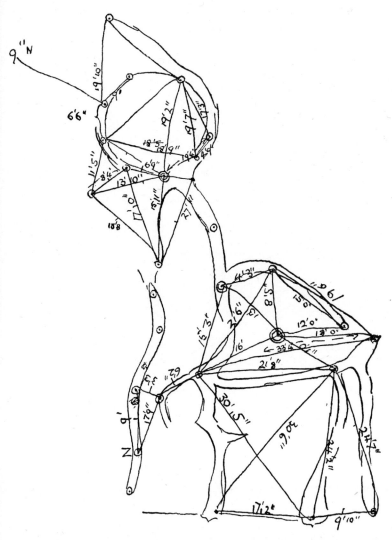

Fig. 3a—Early stages in plotting outlines from sticks.

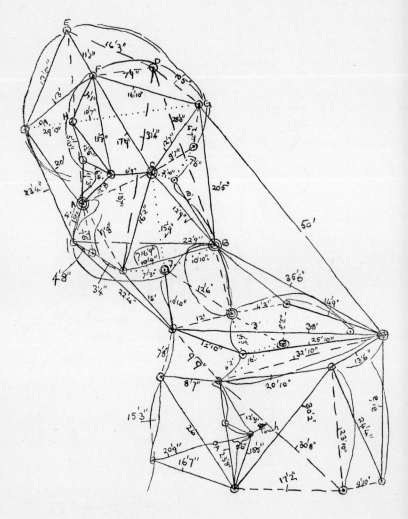

Fig. 3b—Later stage of checking the same outlines. For each fixed point measured here there were about a hundred others. Many other soundings showed no hollows.

scarcely possible to believe. How could anyone know that the
figure was female? Nevertheless events proved them to be
right. Nothing has ever impressed me as being so skilful as
these two identifications. It is true that I was much more practised in the disentangling of Anglo-Saxon art forms; but I was
not entirely lacking in knowledge of those of the Iron Age. To
me the figure was almost meaningless; yet my friends could see
at once what it represented.

It is not necessary to describe the slow unfolding of the picture
of 'Epona' and her amazing horse. For some time it seemed to
me that we might be dealing with some gigantic Romano-
British picture of a cavalryman riding over a fallen savage,
which frequently occurs on Roman tombstones. Until the
giantess's head had been explored, this idea persisted. The
goggle eyes, however, resembling those of the Cerne giant,
began to shake it and when the breasts were found the idea
perished at once. Here was a female giantess, a possibility
which had never occurred to me at the start.

I should mention that it is not possible to appreciate the outlines on the ground. All you can see is a maze of sticks, which
form completely meaningless patterns. When, however, their
position is plotted on paper, the figure begins to form like a
child's magic painting. No one could fake such a figure, because
there is nothing to be seen on the surface of the ground. You
can make mistakes in measurement and mistakes in plotting,
but it is impossible to change the surafce of the chalk rock without removing the turf. As a matter of fact, it seems most unlikely that any living artist could produce such a fantastic
figure on this enormous scale. It must be very far from being
the first attempt at this kind of work (Fig. 4).

To say that the discovery of this female figure was a surprise
is much too mild a description. For one thing, no female hill-
figure was known to exist. For another, it was entirely contrary
to anything which had ever been recorded about the hill. All
reports for the last three hundred years had told of one giant
and that clearly a male. Gervase's tradition spoke of two, or
perhaps three, male figures and a supernatural horse. The
giantess's horse was certainly strange enough to be regarded
as supernatural; but how could the lady's rather benign expres-
sion fit in with the description of two knights locked in battle.

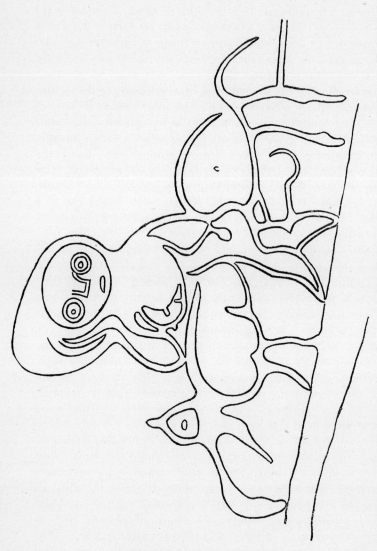

Fig. 4—Figure of the Goddess and her horse as plotted from soundings. It was not expected that the width of the outlines would prove correct when excavated. Length from tip of horse's nose to tip of tail 104 feet.

The only possible explanation seemed to be that, by the time of Gervase, part of the anatomy of the figure had become overgrown and that she had been mistaken for a male figure in a hood. This idea was borne out to some extent by the fact that the lady's hair and the area below her face were very much deeper than the rest of her body. Soundings of nearly three feet in depth were found all over this area. It looked as if special pains had been used to keep it scoured.

If this was the correct explanation, then it seemed possible that the giantess represented the squire in Gervase's tale and was a figure which had been lost since the Middle Ages. And yet Mrs. Rishbeth, Dr. A. C. Haddon's daughter, told me that a chalk pit near the Cambridge Waterworks had been known to her as a child as the print of the hoof of Gogmagog's horse. The chalk pit was apparently of no very great age and therefore it seemed as if a tradition that Gogmagog had a horse had survived, while the figure of it was no longer remembered. The horse could certainly not have been made and become obscured again since the days when William Cole had seen the giant in the first half of the eighteenth century. It is possible that the 'many traditions, since worn away' to which he referred, may have been parts of the horse and giantess so grown up that they looked like letters. This may well have been the case; but it does not explain why only one giant was mentioned by the other writers. If Cole could see things which looked like letters in the turf, they must have been very much clearer in the days of Bishop Hall two hundred years earlier. It is probable, however, that this sentence of Cole's really refers to the wearing away of the giant.

The reason why I say the horse could not have been made since Cole's day, lies in the character of the beast itself. This is no respectable late eighteenth-century animal. It is a weird and completely unnaturalistic beast of a type peculiar to the Celtic Iron Age of western Europe. Such horses with beaks to their faces are first known from the Celts of northern Italy at about 400 B.C. and continued to be represented for the next four hundred years or so. They do not appear to have survived the Roman Conquest of Britain by Claudius' armies, which began in A.D. 43.

It seemed clear to me that the mystery of Gogmagog was not

yet solved. I had found a new figure and not the one that scholars of Cambridge went out to admire. Gogmagog had still to be found.

The obvious thing to do was to return to the soft spots, which had been noticed and marked on the first day of the work. Starting on the one nearest to the hind legs of the horse, it was not long before a second figure began to take shape. It looked very like the original curves of the horse's legs, but in a comparatively short time it resolved itself into a chariot with a pole joining it to the legs of the animal (Fig. 9).

This puzzling find in no way helped to explain Gogmagog, but it did appear to provide an explanation of the traditional buried chariot. Here, sure enough, was a buried chariot, somewhere near the Street, which had once passed from Mutlow Hill towards Wandlebury.

In all other ways, the chariot complicated matters. It did not look as if it were an Iron Age vehicle. It had the appearance of being a chariot of Classical type added to the horse at a later date. The date need not have been much later; but the chariot seemed to be of Roman type, while the horse was entirely of the Iron Age.

Once again I returned to my original marks and began sounding yet another outline. Before doing so, however, it was necessary to test some soft places, which had been observed below the feet of the horse. Here it appeared was a broad band, where the turf had been removed for a width of from 6 to 9 ft. It ran diagonally up the hill in a straight line for more than a hundred yards and appeared to be heading directly for the old entrance of the entrenchment on the top. The horse, lady and chariot had been drawn as if they were on a white road leading up into the earthwork. It seemed hard to avoid the conclusion that this was in fact a roadway and was probably a sacred path heading for something within the earthen ring.

Since Gogmagog still remained coyly in hiding, the only thing to do was to examine the first hollows of all. As before, they soon began to form a curved line, but it had only one side to it. Instead of being a narrow outline, roughly two feet wide, it had an extensive hollow on the far side from the chariot. This was evidently a white figure and not a green one outlined in white.

As it happened, it was not easy to find the far side of the figure. It was much wider than might have been expected. In my first horizontal lines of soundings, I found no opposite side in fifty feet. This was rather discouraging, for I was getting beneath the branches of a clump of beech trees, which might have been surrounded by a ditch when they were planted. I decided to try to hit off the giant's legs. This in itself proved no easy matter. As a matter of fact, there were no actual legs, for the figure is apparently dressed in a long white tunic. The things which did appear, when at last the bar struck firm chalk, were more puzzling than ever. They were small oval, or sausage-shaped, areas and when plotted made no sense at all (Fig. 5). There was one side of a figure reasonably clear and inside it nothing but a confused collection of eight sausages or apples. This is how it appeared to anyone brooding over the chart. The only explanation that I could think of was that this was a picture of the horned Celtic deity, Cernunnos, and that he was pouring the fruits of the earth out of a cornucopia in the manner shown on carvings of the Roman Period found in Gaul (e.g. O. Brogan, *Roman Gaul*, Fig. 47a).

This idea appeared to be borne out when a circular area of firm chalk was found higher up the body, for this might well have been meant to represent the mouth of the cornucopia. At this point everything began to look rather grim. The top portion of the giant was evidently beneath a jungle of very thorny briars, small thorn trees and elm suckers. The roots of these might well have ruined the giant's head. In a few more years the elm roots probably would have done so. However I waded into the jungle with jack-knife and hedging bill, and was delighted to find that the outlines could still be detected. One soon develops a sense of feel with the steel bar and can tell quickly whether the chalk rock is firm, or has been exposed to weathering.

So, although there were a fair number of thorns in my hands and ears by the end of the operations, the head and right arm of the giant could be charted and put on paper.

This giant, 100 ft. high and waving a fifty-foot sword above his head, became a most dramatic personality. His sword at first was not apparently like an Iron Age weapon, but resembled a Roman stabbing sword, a gladius. However I could not be certain of this, for the soundings showed a different kind of filling along the top edge and loose chalk scattered around suggested that I might have hit a modern trench. It was found later that I had hit a modern pipe-line at the upper edge of the sword. The correct shape is shown on the figure. His face, once outlined in green, was ferocious. One knee appeared to be bent; as if he were just about to spring out of the hill, slashing with his sword. I do not know any early picture quite so vigorous as this. It is completely barbaric in feeling and yet is much influenced by the representational art of the Classical world. It is most hard to put a possible date to it (Fig. 5).

At this point, I am afraid curiosity got the better of me. Although it was bound to prolong the labour, I had to know whether or not there was a third figure on the far side of the horse. Mr. C. F. Tebbutt, who made a few soundings with the bar, quickly showed that there was something there. It was clear that the secret of the hill was not to be extracted without many months of hard work. My wrist was already becoming swollen and shaky from the jar of the bar, when it was banged down upon the chalk rock. Still, it is not every year that one has the opportunity of revealing a whole hillside full of Celtic gods.

I had always wanted an independent committee to be formed to prove that my charts were not the product of a disordered mind. However this was not considered practical and I had to deal with the job myself. It was decided therefore to mark out a square on one of the figures and to examine this in the approved archaeological technique. This means that you mark out an area in squares, so that the results fit neatly on to squared paper. Of course, it is not so easy to mark out exact squares on sloping ground as anyone might think. Mercator's Projection, or one of those things, comes into it, and the squares are never square, no matter how hard you try to make them so. None the less, this is the modern technique established by years of archaeological practice. You must mark out your squares before you attempt to do anything. It may seem rather like taking the proverbial hammer to crack a nut, but it is more or less foolproof. The square, or rather rectangle, was duly marked out. It was probably of the same order of accuracy as my original planning. No doubt it was the Fates who decided that one of its corners should

Fig. 5—Figure of Warrior as plotted from soundings and test cuts. Plotting at top half extremely difficult and liable to some error. Height 100 feet.

be fixed on a new soft spot, well away and above the head of
the giantess. The weather then broke and turned to snow.

While the snow lasted, it became difficult to work on the
figure of the swordsman and impossible to excavate either. The
sun thawed out the ground above the giantess's head and it was
possible to continue on that part of the hill. A few days were
enough to show that a huge figure, like a sickle moon, not a
crescent, but a waning moon, extended right up to the top of
the hill. It was thirty-five feet wide between the horns and
more than sixty feet at its longest. Assuming that it was an
essential part of the goddess figure, this gave her a height of
some 120 ft., while the swordsman was only 100 ft.

A new difficulty now appeared, for as the soundings neared
the top of the hill, the chalk rock became progressively deeper
from the surface. It was clear from the feel of it that at some
time an extra foot or so of soil and stones had been dumped just
at the brow of the hill and spread out to form a terrace. This
added very greatly to the difficulty of the task. At two feet, if
the bar hit hard chalk, you could feel it; but if you did not hit
the hard and went on probing to satisfy yourself that it was soft,
it became extremely hard to pull the bar out again. I was not
satisfied with the top left-hand corner of the moon-like shape,
but decided to leave it and examine the ground where it seemed
probable that a third figure lay. It was necessary to try to
establish the full extent of the figures before concentrating on
details.

The third figure (Tebbutt's giant) proved to be the most
difficult of the three. Having been warned, by my examination
of the swordsman, of the tedium of looking for details in a large
white area, it seemed reasonable to try to discover the whole
outline first. Working outwards from the horse's head, the
beginning of an outline was found only two feet distant. There
was no difficulty in running this outline up the hill till it came
within a foot of the giantess's hair and the same distance from
the moon. The outline as plotted was rather a shock, for most of
it closely resembled the side of a gigantic pot. The top, of what
seemed to be the rim, ran within a foot or so of the bottom of
the moon. Here again, however, the soundings suddenly started
to deepen, for I had reached the dump of made-up soil. I left
this for the moment and looked for the opposite side of the

figure at the bottom. Twenty-five feet away I reached hard chalk once again and had no difficulty in following this up to a corner, from which a line appeared to run sideways up the hill and parallel to the opposite side of the thing which looked like a pot. The whole of this line, however, was in the deep soil and I was not satisfied that it had all been plotted correctly.

The chart now appeared to show an enormous jar, tilted sideways up the hill, and fitted into the space between the moon and the giantess's head. At the top, where its left shoulder ought to have been, a large shumack tree made soundings impossible. Since the figure could hardly be expected to be nothing but a 75-ft. pot with human legs, it became necessary to try to locate some outlines of the body which belonged to the legs. It seemed possible that the pot might be resting on the knees of some sitting or reclining figure and so I attempted to find some sign of this to the left. There were areas of soft and hard there; but, when plotted, they showed a series of meaningless curved shapes rising from a white background. The most probable place for the head of the figure was therefore above the thing, which looked like a pot and right in the area of the made-up soil.

The week or so which followed was really rather depressing. At almost every point I sounded the bar went in to a depth of about 2 ft. 6 in. and there stuck. At the end of an hour's work, one was soaked through and very tired. There was clearly a very large area of white and it was almost beyond my strength to sound it all. Something in the nature of an echo sounder was needed. Still, in the end, I hit off hard ground at the top and this swung round in a sweeping curve to near the mouth of the pot. Thinking that this might be some kind of crest to a helmet, or something of that nature, soundings were started again from the line which was thought to be the top side of the jar. A curve of hard ground was found, which ran round inside the top line and appeared to form the framework of a face.

It was now necessary to return to the deep inside of this area in the hope of hitting off some recognizable features. I am afraid I did not like the idea at all. One ought to be about twenty-five years old for this kind of work. However, by making soundings at six-inch intervals, the bar at last hit something solid. This was only about six inches wide and only four feet long. It was sheer misery when it ended and it was really quite heart-breaking to have to start off again in the sticky deeps. All the same, two more similar hard areas were found that afternoon and when I had got home, torn off my wet clothes and plotted my measurements on the chart, I realized that the worst was over. The hard areas were evidently part of a face. They were two eyebrows and a mouth. The next day produced a nose and two minute eyes. These eyes were only about six-inch dots and I did not like to hammer them much with the point of the bar in case they should be too broken up to be re-turfed on clearing the figure (Fig. 10).

The back of the problem was now broken and so was the outline of the fabulous pot. It was no longer necessary to look for a sitting or reclining god. This was a standing one, with huge curves of white lines swirling away from the back of his head. I could only think that it was meant to represent the sun. Close behind him was a goddess with a moon-like face, an object like a waning moon above her head and a jaded horse. She appeared to be the moon herself, who had run her course across the heavens and here was the sun setting out on his daily task. It reminded me of the words of the Nineteenth Psalm: 'In them hath He set a tabernacle for the sun: which cometh forth as a bridegroom out of his chamber, and rejoiceth as a giant to run his course.' What was this figure, but the sun depicted as a giant? Of course the Revised Translation of the Bible reduces him to a 'strong man', but in this case the other words seemed more appropriate. The Greek myth had the sun, Helios, rising from his home near Colchis, at the eastern end of the Black Sea, and driving his chariot westward across the heavens to the Islands of the Bless'd, from whence he returned in a ship to Colchis once again. I had no idea what the carvings on the left of this figure really indicated; but it seemed most likely that they were either part of a chariot, or of a tabernacle. Only further soundings could solve this part of the story, but at least there now appeared to be a possibility of the whole thing making some sense.

A year after the presence of three figures had been established, an account of the discovery of the first two appeared in Canadian newspapers. I then received a letter from Professor F. Heichel-heim of Toronto, whom I had known for many years. He told me that there should be three figures, that one of them ought to be smaller than the other two and that it might be female. This confirmation, deduced from scraps of external information, struck me as being very remarkable.

Work on the third figure was so exhausting that it seemed necessary to find out what really lay beneath the top soil. Why did the bar stick in the places where the figures appeared to have been made? Would it be possible to see anything at all when the outlines were uncovered? It was quite possible that the only change might be a rotting of chalk on exposure to the weather, which might be very hard to observe by eye.

To satisfy myself that I was not wasting time and labour on something which could never be seen, I made six little trial cuts at random spots on the first two discovered figures. The first two, on the horse's rump and on its tail, showed hollows in the chalk filled with ordinary humus. The other four were different. At first sight, when the subsoil was exposed and brushed, you could see little change between the part beneath the supposed outline and the rest of the hillside. A closer study, however, showed that there was a difference. While the ordinary hillside subsoil consisted of little flat slabs of chalk lying horizontally, on the area of the outline the slabs were all uneven and lying on edge at all angles. When examined with a trowel, these were all found to be embedded in a fine, grey, clay-like material. It seemed to be a kind of sludge of powdered chalk, slightly discoloured with humus. It was this sludge which was so tenacious and had prevented the bar from coming out again. All these four cuts showed the same kind of thing. I continued sounding in a more contented frame of mind.

Six months after the work had started, we were able to begin a real excavation. Owing to the discovery of the moon-like figure above the goddess's head, it was decided that this area was altogether too complicated for a start on what was really a new kind of archaeological investigation. We therefore chose the chariot for the experiment. There were no features here which might be damaged and the outline appeared to be reasonably simple; although it had been difficult to determine its limits with any certainty. The area was marked out and divided into ten-foot squares. The first two of these were stripped of turf, leaving a two-foot baulk between them. There would thus be cells ('windows' as they are called) eight-foot square, with turf baulks two-foot wide dividing the excavation up into a grid.

Quite a number of people collected to watch the proceedings. Some were entirely pessimistic; others hopeful. When the sub-soil was reached, it looked exactly the same as it had done in four of the earlier trials. There were gloomy, or satisfied, faces among the onlookers. We knocked off for the day, leaving them to go back to spread alarm and despondency.

The next day I attacked it quite ruthlessly and, as a result, a section could be seen, which showed up the outline just where it had been indicated by the bar, but considerably wider. It was a very shallow depression in the chalk rock, with a smooth floor and weathered sides resembling the top layers of an old chalk pit. It was like a hollow, which had been open for a long time and had filled with rain-washed, powdered chalk sludge. This was not the interpretation placed on it by other observers. I had to pacify indignant countrymen, who thought that their lifelong experience had been belittled by armchair critics. One Continental sage was of the opinion that everything was the result of frost action. I did not entirely disagree. You cannot expose a chalk surface for centuries to the action of water and frost without appreciable change. It was, in fact, just such a change that I was hoping to be able to observe. This was not a question of searching for ditches which had been deliberately dug and later filled in; it was one of looking for places where turf had been removed to show a white picture and where frost and rain had broken up the surface, which might have had to be scraped from time to time to free it from grass and weeds. The excavation appeared to show just this kind of thing.

An interesting sidelight on the mentality of to-day appeared when I came to measure in the grid to fit it on the original plan. Several fixed measuring sticks, which were rather more obvious than their neighbours, were found to have been deliberately pulled out and thrown aside. This was obviously intended to be a nuisance. As a matter of interest, it only took a few minutes to replace them. There were too many fixed points for any hooligan to be bothered to remove them all. Still, it leaves that unpleasant taste in one's mouth, which we must expect so long as children are not brought up to a sense of responsibility and discipline.

While the excavations were going on, I suddenly became possessed of a very welcome piece of information. Mrs. V. Pritchard has been collecting a series of rubbings of pictures scratched on the walls of churches. This study, which was first brought to our knowledge by the celebrated Medievalist, the late Dr. Coulton, has been belittled by many scholars, who appeared to regard it as of a trivial character. One gets quite accustomed to this kind of approach to any new branch of study and it hurts nothing but the reputation of the opposition.

Mrs. Pritchard's work was already providing convincing proofs of its value. In the days when paper was not available, and parchment was very expensive, the smooth surface of the chalk blocks in the interior of a church provided something on which you could draw, or scribble down notes. Drawings and short inscriptions are found in most of our local churches. Although many are of a trivial character, they are not in the same class as the obscene scribblings in public lavatories of to-day and some are very interesting indeed. For instance, one feels a close link with the past when someone writes that this year Sir Francis Drake sailed round the world. One can almost see the man, in his slashed doublet, laboriously scratching it with the point of his knife. Round was the important word. Nobody in this country had been quite sure that it really was round, till the anchor splashed down from the cat-head of the *Golden Hind*. Others may have been round it before; but who believed the words of people who spoke a different language. Here was one of our own people, who had brought his own ship right round the whole thing. It was something worth commemorating in the most permanent place in the community, whatever parson might think about it.

Now, it seemed to me most remarkable that no one at any time had left a picture of the Wandlebury figures. No antiquary had apparently done so and no artist had added them to the curiosities of eastern England. Yet, one at any rate had been famed over a wide area. I felt it was most probable that some-one at some time might have felt inclined to scratch a picture of them on the wall of some church. Therefore I showed Mrs. Pritchard the plan of our figures and asked her whether she had ever seen anything in the least like any of them. To my great disappointment, the answer was 'No'.

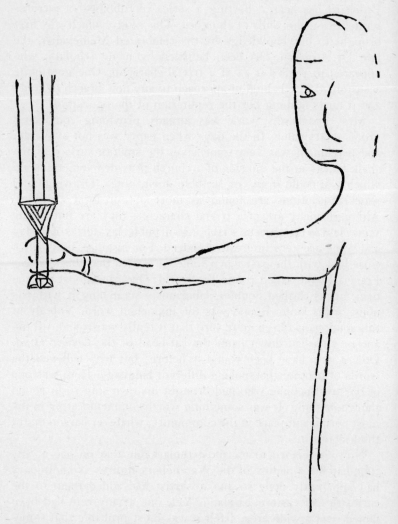

Fig. 6—Figure, fifteen inches high, scratched on a pillar in Sawston Church.

Some time later, however, she rang me up to say that, on going through her collection of rubbings, she had found one figure of a man apparently holding a sword—one only, it seems, from the whole district. On asking where it was, the reply was quite exciting. The figure was on a pillar in Sawston church. Sawston was the only clue to the location of the giants in the first instance. It was not long before we were on our way to look for it.

There were many things scratched on the Norman pillars of the church. Some were modern indecencies; others probably almost as old as the columns themselves. The figure of the man was rather above normal eye level and about fifteen inches high. It was roughly, but not too badly, drawn and was clearly of considerable age. It represented a man in a tunic, which concealed his feet, holding what seemed to be a two-edged sword, with no point, in his extended right hand (Fig. 6). More trouble had been taken over the drawing of the hand and hilt of the sword than over anything else. The remarkable thing was that the hilt was quite unlike any medieval or later weapon. It was completely without a cross guard, or quillons, and had a most unmedieval pommel. Yet the man was dressed in a long tunic and could hardly have belonged to any period later than the Middle Ages, or an even earlier date.

The coincidences seemed almost too numerous. Here, in the church of the one village from which it was known that the giant was visible about a hundred years ago, was the only known picture of a warrior in the area. He was dressed like our giant and was holding a sword of a type not known later than the Saxon Period in Britain. Just beyond the sword was an extremely rough drawing of the hindquarters of a horse. It was all too much to be an accident. Somebody, perhaps two people, had tried to draw two of our figures from memory. There was no other way of doing it, for there was no paper on which to make a preliminary sketch. One could not expect great accuracy in detail. The sword might be held at shoulder level and not above his head; but it was a broadsword of an archaic type. The symbolism of the cross on the medieval sword-hilt was too important for anyone to forget it at that time. The omission of the guard was deliberate. The figure was dressed in the same kind of long tunic as the giant. If this was not an attempt to draw our giant, it was little short of a miracle.

Near the foot of this swordsman in Sawston church there is an inscription. No one has yet been able to read it. I have no idea whether it concerns the figure or not. The very fact that it is there and as yet untranslated will serve to show how one's curiosity is kept alive all through an investigation of this kind. A story slowly unfolds, which is quite unlike the one expected at the beginning. Where one hoped to find a single male figure, there are now two males, a female, a horse and a chariot. From week to week there is no real clue as to what is coming next. From month to month one's only link with reality has been a steel bar, which would go deeper into the ground in some places than in others and one's only idea of the meaning of this has been the slow growth of unexpected figures, resulting from the plotting of measurements on paper. This is certainly the strangest investigation that I am ever likely to undertake and, in some ways, it is even more exciting than the excavation of ancient Eskimo houses in Ellesmere Land, with the pack ice slowly drifting down to cut us off from the ship. There is no need to go to the ends of the earth for interesting quests and excitement. It is here, anywhere in prosaic old England, at one's back door. You will never get the full enjoyment out of it, however, unless you are ready to jump at once to any clue and forget all the careful plans and preparations with which you started. Again and again I have seen clues, which might have led to thrilling discoveries, shelved and not followed up, because they did not fit in with the well-ordered plan of work to be carried out. I have seen too the chance of a really great adventure thrown away, because somebody wanted to make just one more scientific experiment, which in fact was never made.

Chapter Three

NOT long after this I began to notice from the faces of other archaeologists, that they were seriously disturbed by my interpretation of the excavation. It was clear that they neither believed in the outlines, nor understood what they were to expect. I had been rather puzzled myself by some features, which appeared when the turf was removed. Although from the age of six I had been a haunter of chalk pits for one reason or another, I had never seen the surface of the chalk rock looking at all like the surface now exposed. It was remarkably smooth and very hard. The normal section of the top of any chalk formation is quite different. There you see the top soil, or humus, slowly changing into tiny rounded bits of chalk, then into small blocks and so into larger blocks, till at last you reach solid unbroken rock. Nobody I consulted could explain it; although one geologist said at once that it was abnormal and that the top chalk must have been removed. That was what I thought myself; but the only explanation that occurred to me at the time was that the whole thing had been deliberately skinned of turf, the loose chalk removed and the turf then replaced to form the figures. This was quite wrong.

Since the others could have no first-hand knowledge of what I had learnt with the bar, it seemed that the only easy way of showing them that the outlines were really there was to demonstrate that they coincided with what had been planned on some complicated feature of the pattern. Although there was a risk of doing some damage, I therefore chose the goddess's face as being both complicated and relatively obvious. No one could possibly create a pair of eyes and a nose beneath the turf. Either the chalk would appear different where they had been plotted, or the whole thing was a mirage of some remarkable

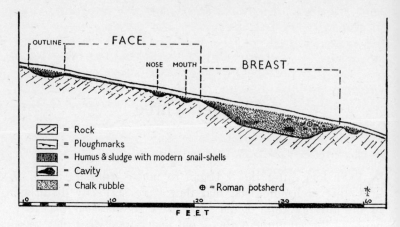

Fig. 7a—Section over upper half of Goddess.

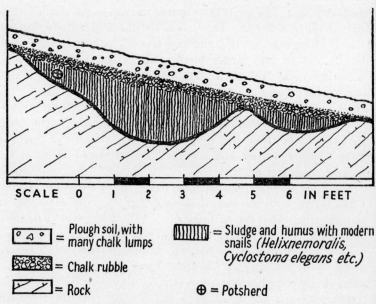

Fig. 7b—Section at the junction of the Goddess's hair with the outline of her face (the hollow on the right).

kind. Therefore I ran two trenches at right angles across the goddess's left eye with one passing over the right eye.

As soon as these trenches reached the chalk rock and its surface had been brushed, two things were clear. First the chalk rock was quite different where the eyes were supposed to be. Secondly the marks made by ploughshares were clearly visible in the rock itself. The ring of the left eye, as had been observed in other cuts of the outlines, was filled with grey sludge. When examined with a trowel, part of the filling appeared to lie in an actual and man-made hollow in the chalk, while part was rotted chalk into which the mud had soaked. Mud would have collected, of course, in the ring after rain and especially after the thaw of a heavy snowfall. I had often seen similar material formed in cart ruts in grassy lanes in winter. To me it was so ordinary and so obvious that I was quite amazed to find that other archaeologists could not see it at all.

They did not believe that there was a figure there. It was exactly like the kind of situation you meet in a dream. You come down to breakfast after a good wash and shave. Someone at the table says, 'You haven't shaved this morning, Tom.' You reply, 'Of course I have. I always do, even in the train.' They say, 'I'll prove you haven't shaved.' They go out and return with a very old barber. He looks at you and says, 'I don't really know whether you have shaved or not, but if I were you I'd go and buy a new razor.' Then he gets up and goes away to fiddle with a clock on the mantelpiece. The next day, feeling no cause to buy a new razor, you think, after what has been said, that it would be as well to put in a new razor-blade. This gives you a splendid shave and you come down to breakfast as smooth as a porpoise. At once the tiresome fellow says again, 'You haven't shaved this morning.' 'Very well,' you reply in great irritation, 'I'll prove to you that I've shaved. My shaving brush must be still wet. Come up and look at it.' The man looks at it suspiciously and says nothing. Your wife looks over your shoulder and says, 'Of course he has shaved. Look at all those dirty prickles round the edge of the basin, which he has been too careless to wash out.' The man looks blankly at the prickles and remarks, 'Nevertheless, I cannot see the slightest proof that he has shaved.' What are you to do in such a situation?

It took me some time to think out what was bothering them.

They had never used the bar themselves and they had little
knowledge of chalk. They were expecting to see an ordinary
archaeological phenomenon of a ditch in the chalk, filled with
brown soil. It wasn't there, therefore there could not be any
figure. Furthermore they appeared to think that there was
something brilliant and remarkable about the whole thing. They
were landsmen and quite unable to think in terms of a seaman's
training, where the lead line is one of the most elementary
guides to navigation. I was so used to thinking in terms of
charts, that I had not realized that soundings, bearings and so
on were a closed book to others. But why were there no ditches?
Well, that was easy enough. They had been ploughed off. All
that remained was the mud and rot at the bottom, in the chalk
rock, which was too hard for the plough to break up and turn
into humus.

I was working there quietly one afternoon, when I felt something watching me. Just as I once felt an old dog-fox watching
me, when I was fishing for small brown trout in an Exmoor
coomb, with a line on the end of a walking stick. I looked up
slowly to find two local farmers, whom I knew, watching me
quite silently. This was what was wanted. I asked them whether
they ever ploughed into the chalk. Of course they did on poor
land. Sometimes they ploughed off an inch a year. What was
the grey sludge? It was rotted chalk where the turf had been
taken off and rain and frost had got at the subsoil. They were
prepared to go to court and swear to it. This was really all I
wanted to know, except how much chalk was missing. This was
important, for it might give some idea of the original depth of
the outlines. The answer might be found in a study of the exposed
faces of neighbouring chalk pits.

There used to be an old pit within a quarter of a mile of the
giants; but when I got there, after not seeing it for fifteen years,
it had all fallen in. The next one was still within half a mile of
the figures, on the same chalk formation and the same range of
hills. I slithered into it and made an examination (Fig. 8).
The section was regular and clear. First there came about a foot
of soil and humus. Then an inch layer of tiny grains of chalk,
about a quarter of an inch in diameter. These are known as
'pea chalk' and are found on the bottom of most man-made
cuttings in the local chalk. You find them at the bottom of

Plotting the figures with bar and sticks
(The goddess' head is on the right of the picture)

[Photo: The Evening News]

Pl. II

A. Excavation of goddess' head. Turf replaced
B. Later stage of excavation. Breast area cleared except one baulk.
Horse's head begun in distance

graves and ditches. They are often supposed to be the work of worms. Below the pea chalk was eleven inches of chalk broken into layers of blocks. These were half an inch or so wide at the top and graded down to those an inch and a half at the bottom. They were perfectly regularly disposed in horizontal layers. Beneath this there was three inches of rather larger blocks some two and a half inches wide. Finally came unbroken and very hard rock.

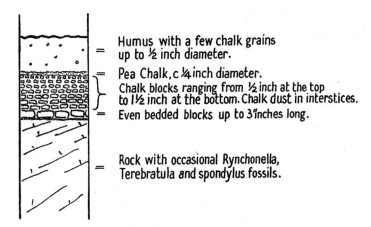

Humus with a few chalk grains up to ½ inch diameter.

Pea Chalk, c ¼ inch diameter.

Chalk blocks ranging from ½ inch at the top to 1½ inch at the bottom. Chalk dust in interstices.

Even bedded blocks up to 3 inches long.

Rock with occasional Rynchonella, Terebratula and spondylus fossils.

Fig. 8—Control Section from chalk pit to half a mile west of Giants.
    These two sections demonstrate the very heavy ploughing which has taken place on the giants. All the chalk blocks have been ploughed off and some remain in the soil above. Much humus has washed down the slope.

(*same scale as* 7b.)

On the figures there was nothing like this. First there was about nine inches of plough soil, full of lumps of chalk of varying sizes. Then an inch or so of small chalk lumps; then came either bare chalk rock, or one layer of the larger two and a half inch blocks. The plough marks, roughly nine inches apart, were two inches or so deep in the chalk rock itself. Since the pit and the giants were on the same kind of rock and close together on the same line of hills, it seemed pretty certain that both had once been the same. Not less than a foot of chalk blocks had been ploughed away. It might have been a few inches more. This was

E   49

why there were no ditches to be seen on the outlines. They had been ploughed clean off. It also explained the marked difference between the soundings in the outlines and those outside. Since the surface had been reduced to the hardest chalk rock, the bar would not go into it, as it might have done had the broken blocks remained to any depth. But it would go into the rotten areas, where the removal of the turf had allowed frost and rain to work for centuries. As a matter of fact there were shallow ditches of two or three inches in places, but that was just a bit of luck. All visible signs might easily have been ploughed away.

It seems then that the outlines of the goddess's head had once been of the order of some fifteen inches in the chalk. Perhaps they were a bit less, but not much more. The outlines of the Cerne giant are about two feet deep in the chalk. It is perhaps softer than ours and has been exposed probably for a longer time. There is, in fact, no evidence that two of our figures have been seen since the days of Gervase of Tilbury and then they may have already disappeared; for all he did was to quote a tradition of before his own time at the end of the twelfth century. Assuming that the Cerne and Wandlebury figures are more or less contemporary, and date from about the time of the Birth of Christ, Cerne has been exposed for a much longer time and its outlines would in any case be deeper. Thus, if both chalks were subject to more or less the same rate of rot, we might even make a rough calculation and say that, as the Cerne outlines are about twenty-four inches deep and have reached that depth in about nineteen hundred years, then, since our outlines were about fifteen inches deep, they were open for about eleven hundred and eighty years. But Gervase of Tilbury left England in about A.D. 1177. This is rather an interesting coincidence. It is much too unreliable of course to be taken with any seriousness; but it is remarkable nevertheless. I was inclined to believe that the horse goddess was last cleaned before Gervase of Tilbury went overseas. Since he only speaks of what I have assumed to be the figures as an ancient tradition, this coupled with the rough-and-ready evidence from the ground itself, strongly suggested that the figures were no more than a memory in Gervase's day. Or at least that some of them were not easy to recognize.

The question of why there should be a clear division between the broken-up chalk and the solid rock is rather interesting.

Many people think that it is just a matter of water percolating down through the cracks. In other words, that it is due to rain falling on the land above. If this were so, we would be able to observe humus in the fissures of the chalk, right down to the solid rock. Instead of this, the cracks between the blocks are filled with chalk dust with no trace of brown from the soil. In our local chalk at any rate, the brown humus does not penetrate far into the cracks. I think it is necessary to look for the explanation a long time ago. Probably the origin of the jointing is to be found in glacial conditions.

Now, in the Arctic one finds that, although a foot or so of the surface soil is thawed out in summer and is often completely loose and fairly dry, yet below this layer you come suddenly on another layer which is never thawed. There is enough frozen water in it to make it almost impervious to anything less forceful than gelignite. I have tried for half an hour to chip an old Eskimo toy boat out of this frozen ground and, although I managed to do it in the end with a miner's pick, one might just as well have been chipping it out of granite. This layer of permanent ice must have been found here also during the Ice Age. The summer heat would have lasted longer than it does in the Arctic today and would have penetrated further into the ground; but you would still find that layer iron-bound with ice.

This, I think, must be the answer. Above the solid, frozen chalk rock there would have been many inches, which expanded and contracted yearly with the cold and heat. The contraction broke the chalk into separate blocks and the expansion pressed them together. The frost powdered their edges. Such water as penetrated from above, in winter formed a skin of ice round each block and the flaking off was greater where there was more water near the top. Many people must have seen loose blocks of chalk covered with this icy skin. They are reduced in size by flaking very rapidly.

This process, rather than ordinary solution of the chalk by percolating water, seems to me to be the most likely explanation of the facts. Water seeping through, for perhaps ten thousand years, has no doubt added to the reduction in size of the blocks; but I think they were already broken up during the Glacial Period, and this aided very considerably a rapid spread of plant life, directly arctic conditions were removed. There

were the fissures, ready made, in which seeds could germinate
and plants grow. In the Arctic plants grow wherever there is the
slightest encouragement for them to do so. I have located
several ancient Eskimo villages from the sea, simply because
vegetation can grow better on the richer soil derived from the
rubbish thrown away by their inhabitants. Just as you can locate
many ancient sites round our windswept coasts by the nettles
growing on the old rubbish dumps; so you can pick out an old
Eskimo village, within ten degrees of the North Pole, by the
grass growing on its ruins. Everything else may be as naked as
a slagheap outside a coalmine, but the Eskimo village can be
seen from three miles out to sea, as a green spot in a grey
wilderness. It may be nearly a thousand years old. Behind it are
the mountains under their deep white mantle. Before it is un-
melted ice still fast to the rocks on the edge of the sea. Outside
is the glittering, drifting mass of floating 'pack' and the wan-
dering bergs. All other indents and bays are as naked as a tarmac
road. The site of the ancient village itself, however, is nearly as
green as a salt marsh in summer.

The excavation of the goddess was a slow business. Scarcely
anything was done for about four months in the summer of
1955. In the autumn, however, work began again. The large
curved band of grey, hardened sludge beneath the goddess's
chin, which many people had believed to have been formed in
the glacial period, was shown to dip steeply into a pit-like
depression, which formed the figure's breast. On top of the
sludge, weathered chalk, lumps of turf and ordinary earth, with
snail shells in it, had been tipped at some time or other. The
whole central area of the breast was about three feet beneath
the modern ground level and the filling material had been
tipped on to it at a time when it had been scraped clean and
white at the bottom. Judging by the condition of the rest of the
outlines, it seems probable that the figure was deliberately
filled in and effaced at a time when it was only partly cleaned.
One speculates whether the customary festivities, which accompanied the scouring of such figures, had proved too much for
the sensibilities of some new owner of the land and he had
angrily ordered it to be filled in at once.

It appeared probable also that this breast area had never consisted of simple outlines like the rest of the figure; but had

Fig. 9—Plan of the excavations of the Wandlebury Goddess. Lightly dotted areas indicate grass. Broken lines show general position of outlines sounded by the bar. The excavated portions are shaded for light coming from the south-east. Where no grass is shown at the top left-hand side of the goddess' hair, the figure touches Tebbutt's giant. The round object in the goddess' left hand is thought to be an 'Apple of Life'.

always been stripped completely of turf. At least one breast appears to have been deliberately moulded in the chalk and there appear to be three breasts formed by the pit area and one outside it, shown only in outline (Fig. 9). It is not easy to be sure of this, for when a figure has been exposed to rain and frost for hundreds of years and subjected to periodical scrapings, changes must occur in the original design. It looks as if the goddess had four breasts, but this is not certain. It is clear, however, that no possible trick of the Glacial Period could have made and filled this in. Since the sludge is precisely the same in the breast and in the other outlines, it is hard to see how an Ice theory can be maintained. As Dr. Margaret Murray remarked, after staring steadfastly at the form, which was emerging from the hillside, 'So people think that was made by the ice, do they? Very clever of the ice!'

I think myself that much of the material, which was used to fill the figure in, was taken from the heap of scourings and old turf, which came originally from the figures themselves. The chalk, which had been thrown back into it, had been long exposed to frost and weather and was no longer in sharp angular blocks. It was so sticky when it went in that the passage of farm implements over it had hardened its surface, till it could hardly be moved with a spade. Yet the bar went clean through it with ease; although it cannot be driven an inch into the undisturbed rock. On top of it was a layer of the pea chalk, which so many archaeologists have been taught to regard as the bottom of everything. Some inches beneath this pea chalk, Mr. Hopkin found a fragment of grey Romano-British or Belgic pottery.

Below the goddess's breast, the back of her horse was found to be rather wider than it had been planned. It had been scoured a foot into the chalk rock. Here a phenomenon was observed, which has also been noted on the Uffington White Horse. The bottom of the outline was filled with the grey sludge (I call it grey, but perhaps grey-brown would be a better term), but above the sludge were some inches of broken chalk lumps, which had been pressed into the top of it. This explained the phenomenon I had observed in my earliest sections. Rather than go to the trouble of scraping all the sludge out of the bottom, some scourers of the figure had filled the outlines with fresh chalk on top of the dirt at the bottom. Had no bar been used in the first place, archaeologists looking at a stripped surface of the hill, by eye alone, might easily have failed to recognize any figure at all. This can happen to anybody. I have dug right over graves without seeing them in a Romano-British cemetery at Guilden Morden and a Saxon one at Burwell. These graves have shown up later, when rain fell on the cleared chalk surface. Many things probably have been missed in this way. Pea chalk, brushing and so on are all useful guides; but they are not by any means infallible. Pea chalk is the least valuable of any. It will form on anything hard enough to prevent the passage of worms where there is chalk in the humus, which passes through the worm's inside. There will be plenty of it in the real bottom of a grave or ditch, simply because the worms can go no deeper.

About Christmas time in 1955, while my amateur helpers were involved in the festivities formerly associated with Sol Invictus, I was able to spend some more time on 'Tebbutt's' giant. For some reason, perhaps because my hands were harder, I did not find it so laborious as I had done at the beginning of the year. This was clearly the correct season for this task, because it soon became evident that it was indeed a figure of the sun. Plunging boldly into the area, which had once seemed to look like a gigantic pot, it was not long before the bar struck solid chalk once more. On tracing this, which proved to be a narrow ribbon, scarcely more than a foot wide, I had a new surprise. The ribbon plotted out as a huge, half-opened wing, fifty-four feet long and twenty feet wide. The top of it had actually been charted before by Tebbutt when we were working on the outline of the pot-like shape. Now it fitted at once into a reasonable picture. But I had never thought of finding a wing.

Speculations on the possible position of an arm and on what it could be holding, had taken up a lot of thought. A wing, however, was quite unexpected. Somehow I had never imagined a flying sun and had expected him to be getting into a chariot to make his journey through the sky. Still, here he was, just opening his wings, so my wife thought, to rise up from the hill into the air (Fig. 10).

The more I worked on his outline, the more grand the general design appeared to be. Great rays of white, separated by thin bands of solid chalk, which had once shown green, spread backwards from his forehead and curled round the edges of the goddess's moon. The sun was evidently portrayed as rising behind the waning moon. Some great artist had worked this design out. It was far beyond the conception of any ordinary

Fig. 10—Thought to represent Sun God. Charting not complete.

man. A figure one hundred and seventeen feet high and eighty-five feet broad had been planned with remarkably true curves on a hillside, whose slope varied and was nowhere steep enough to give a good idea of what was being drawn on it. The design seems to have been drawn on a small scale first and produced on the hill by measurement. This was probably the work of a man who could use the equivalent of pencils, rulers, compasses and paper, and not of somebody standing on a distant hill and shouting directions for the movement of rods, or flags, on the slope by eye. The whole thing suggested civilization and education and was of quite a different order to that of the goddess. This was true also of the giant with the sword. He was barbaric, but he was not so unconventional and primitive as the Lady. She was of the very essence of Celtic Art; the two gods owed something to the Classical World. Yet they were not Roman in character. They had a force and originality entirely of their own. Somebody, I think he makes our modern artists look pretty small, had welded the whole thing into one great picture, a hundred yards long and thirty yards high. Furthermore, people had been persuaded to dig this picture into the hill. It was on a cathedral scale. Only very strong religious convictions could have ordered its construction.

I have spent a lot of time just sitting in a chair and looking at the plan of the soundings spread out on the floor. I find it hard to believe that this has actually happened. It is no surprise to me that trained archaeologists, who had seldom touched a bar in their lives, should have found it difficult to believe that such a thing could be revealed in this way. Friends have suggested that some kind of planchette directed the bar: others have hinted that the thing was faked. I do not blame them. I expected it. I have, however, offered the bar to sceptics and have seen their faces. I do not wish to be unkind, but I am afraid it needs some muscle to wield the thing and many hours of toil to do the job. There must be many thousand bar holes on that hill, not less than thirty thousand.

Fortunately I was warned to publish a plan before beginning excavation.[1] Otherwise people might have said that I was making the giants as they were dug out. I have also taken care to have witnesses to the proceedings and to get them to do some of the work. It proved impossible for observers to deny that there was a difference in the chalk where the bar showed such a difference to exist. It was also clear that such a difference had nothing to do with the Ice Age, but was due to man's interference with the hill. Fragments of Roman pottery were found, here and there, in the bottoms of the outlines.

[1] *Archaeological News Letter*, 1955.

As Mr. M. C. Burkitt, the Founder of the Cambridge School of Archaeology, pointed out, it is really of no importance what is found in the bottoms of the outlines, provided they conform to the chart of the soundings. They might contain glacial material, Roman pottery, bully beef tins or chewing-gum. If they are in the shapes shown by the chartings, no agency other than man could have been responsible for their construction. The excavations show that wherever the bar indicated soft ground, it can be observed when the turf is stripped. The trenches were there and then they were filled in. That is all. Every few feet the rotted stumps of the original artichoke stalks were visible in the fillings, showing that we were on the same lines.

And so the figures are really there and no one is more surprised at them than I am myself. Neither planchette, Ice Age, nor rain-water gullies can explain away these remarkable things.

I do not for a moment believe that they are unique. Their skilful construction argues the former existence of many more; only the very largest of which, the Cerne giant, the Long Man of Wilmington and the Uffington White Horse have survived. There must have been a host of them in Europe and plenty in Britain. More could almost certainly be found and at least I hope to hear one day of the recovery of the Red Horse of Tysoe and the Giant on Shotover Hill at Oxford.

One other White Horse is always said to have been destroyed by a Mr. Gee in the late eighteenth century. This horse stood on the hillside below the Iron Age fort of Bratton, near Westbury. Mr. Gee, with such an appropriate surname, constructed a new white horse, which can be seen, shining white, from the train today. But Gee did not destroy the older horse. When you come to think of it, how would you destroy a white horse? You would surely fill it in. If you wish to make another, you would not muddle about in trenches which were already there, but lay out your picture on a fresh stretch of turf, like using a new sheet of paper. The old Bratton horse can be seen quite plainly on the air photograph in Marples' book on white horses. From this I have sketched what I can see of it. It looks very much as if it were a 'beaked' horse of Iron Age type. It is so close to Gee's new horse that there would be no difficulty in opening it up again. I do not consider, therefore, that the Bratton horse is missing. (Fig. 13.)

Why nobody has remarked on this before, I cannot imagine. Hundreds of people must have looked at this air photograph, but they have been plainly told that the older horse was destroyed. Either their curiosity was not strong enough to make them look for themselves, or the power of the printed word is so great that they never thought of looking. In this way many erroneous beliefs became fast fixed in the world of learning. It is exactly the same with this business of 'pea' chalk. Somebody thought that pea chalk was only found at the very bottom of excavations and published this as a fact. Hundreds believed it and never thought of looking to see whether it was true. In many cases it is true; in others it is not.

It is just the same with the bar. No farmer in the west in my boyhood would have dreamt of wasting time and money trenching a damp field to look for choked drains. It was far easier to put on a man in the damp places to probe for the missing pipes. I have watched it being done many times. Yet archaeologists, having been brought up to think that everything must be dug, regarded the use of the bar as a kind of mysterious rite.

Before I leave this part of the story, I should perhaps say that any geological explanation of the outlines of the figures, which involves their construction and filling under arctic conditions, is quite out of the question. Geological formations are mostly dated by the fossils found in them. From the sludge fillings of the outlines, beneath a layer of fresh chalk laid on this sludge, we recovered numerous 'fossils'. These are the shells of a common land-snail, *Helix nemoralis*, which is particularly fond of feeding on nettles and rather lush vegetation. It must be well known to most people as a globular, yellowish snail with black bands. There is no food for such a snail in arctic conditions. The climate when the outlines filled up was similar to what it is to-day. Before the outlines were re-whitened, nettles and lush vegetation were growing in parts of them. The sludge continued to wash out from the grassy sides of the outlines and covered the empty snail shells to various depths.

Chapter Four

IT is now possible to return to Gervase and his story. We have charted our hillside and the chart is nearly completed. Gervase's story, as we have seen in the beginning of this account, was of a fight in the moonlight at the Wandlebury earthwork. A Norman baron, Osbert FitzHugh, rode or drove up to the camp, challenged a mysterious knight to fight, defeated him and, in accordance with the customs of medieval duelling, handed over the enemy's captured horse to a squire. They returned to Cambridge with their prize; but not before Osbert had been slightly wounded by the unknown warrior.

Now, if we look at the complete chart (Fig. 11a), there are three figures, a moon, a horse and a chariot. The horse is so queer that anyone might regard it as being supernatural. One of the figures is certainly a warrior; but he carries a round shield, which was not a Norman fashion. The lumps and blobs on his body suggest that he is wounded and bleeding freely. I take this figure to be the unknown knight. The moon is there already. It may be a curious shape in the plan, but this hill slope flattens out on its upper half. The smallest figure we now know to be female. At a distance, however, when it was grass grown and seen by medieval eyes, it might well have been taken for a half-grown male figure in a hood. I believe the goddess to have been Gervase's traditional squire.

The third giant, which I believe to represent the Sun God, would also appear in a different light to Normans who saw it for the first time. The half-folded wing would seem to them to be a picture of one of their own kite-shaped shields, being worn on the appropriate left arm of a knight. Both knights wear tunics down to the ground. These probably represent the Celtic 'leinie', but to Normans they would be mail hawberks. The rays from the sun's head would seem like plumes on a helmet. There is even a small raised shape near the point of the wing to be explained as blood from an unnoticed wound. What this really represents, I cannot think. I suppose it might conceivably be intended as a feather falling from the wing as it was opened. It seems quite clear to me that the sun figure has become Osbert FitzHugh in Gervase's tale.

Now if this is the right explanation, and it conforms to Inherent Probability, we can date the origin of Gervase's story within fairly narrow limits. It is only necessary to look at the Bayeux Tapestry to see warriors armed with both round and kite-shaped shields.[1] The Normans had given up the round shield by the time of their invasion of England in A.D. 1066, because they had become cavalry men. The kite-shaped shield gave much greater protection for their legs on horseback. I have little doubt that the Normans would have regarded our sword-waver as bearing out-of-date weapons. He might be taken for an English ghost knight. The wraith of someone like Hereward, who was still holding the Isle of Ely in A.D. 1070.

This is one point: the other is just as important. The people who made up the story did not know who the figures were. They knew no names and simply invented a tale to fit a phenomenon, which they could see on the hill when they rode out from Cambridge castle. But if the story was made up soon after the Conquest, they would not have known who the figures were because they were French speakers, while the local population spoke Anglo-Saxon. This then is the explanation of why there is no mention of Gogmagog in Gervase's tale. The people, who told him the story as a traditional one a hundred years after the Conquest, did not know of God and Magog in this connection.

There is no need to assume any longer that the name Hogmagog or Gogmagog was a recent application in Elizabethan times. It had been there all along, but in Gervase's day it had not yet been learnt by the ruling caste. It was still known locally less than fifty years ago and it was still in its original form of Gog and Magog.

One other point can be inferred from Gervase. There were three figures in his story. This shows clearly that the Sun and Moon had not been filled in as a result of Cnut's law against the

[1] F. R. Fowke, *The Bayeux Tapestry*, G. Bell and Sons, 1915, Pl. lxviii.

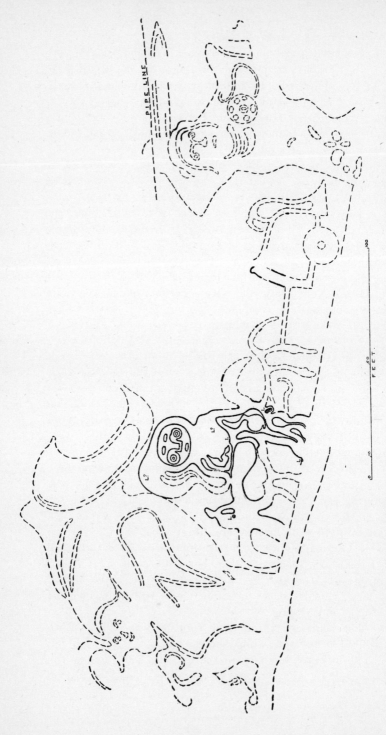

Fig. 11a—Complete chart of Wandlebury figures. Excavated areas surrounded by continuous heavy line. Sounded areas in broken line. L—Libation pit. The three on the upper part of the goddess

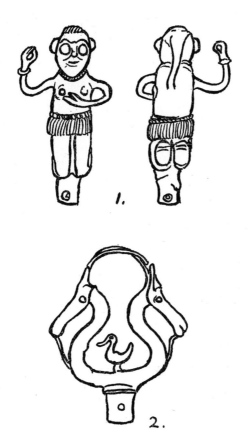

Fig. 11b—Bronze figurines from Faardal, Funen. (After Hans Kjaer.)
    1. Mother Goddess (2·65 inches)
    2. Horses and bird (5 inches)
    Suppose date about 400 B.C.

worship of Sun and Moon in the eleventh century. Since too, there were ceremonies of such a nature at Wandlebury, in the days of the Tudors, that the University Senate had to take steps to discourage their members from attending them, it seems reasonably clear that the three figures had not been filled in at that time. Yet only one is mentioned in A.D. 1605. Perhaps the University ban led to some cessation in the process of scouring. It may well have been the undergraduates who kept the old custom alive.

Some research at Oxford might produce useful evidence about the Shotover Hill Giant, which seems to have gone out of use at the time of the Civil War. Was it the enthusiasm of Oxford undergraduates which kept it scoured till that time? There is no reason to suppose that we are yet at the end of possible lines of investigation into these matters.

The comparison between the reality and the concocted story told by Gervase, may help us in future research into tales elsewhere. It is clear that, in our case, the story was constructed from visual evidence. A great picture could be seen on the hill and a tale had to be made up to account for it. The actual tale has no bearing on the original purpose of the figures, but it does tell us how many were there and give some idea of what they seemed to be doing. This may be the clue to how such stories should be treated. The witches associated with some spring will perhaps have been goddesses formerly worshipped there. The giant, Hiccafrith, was a visible figure with wheel and club. He is still associated with a particular spot because that is where his rites were enacted.

It seems evident that there must have been at least two giants on Plymouth Hoe, not because it is thought that a new one may have been made, but because Geoffrey of Monmouth tells of two contestants in a wrestling match.

It is necessary at this point to say something more detailed about the figures themselves. The first thing, that strikes anyone who is interested in drawing when shown the whole group of figures at Wandlebury, is that the warrior and the sun god are not drawn by the same man as the goddess. The whole character of the picture is different. Whereas the goddess is a completely symbolic figure, with no attempt at representing human and animal forms exactly; the other gods are much more

General view of site at early stage

Two squares open on chariot on right. Goddess in middle. Horse's head begun on left

Pl. IV

[*Photo: The Times*

Air photo of goddess partly excavated

The baulk shown in Pl. II B runs from top to bottom of the white area below the face. Horse's

naturalistic. They are meant to be seen looking like men. Where she is shown in broken outline; they are drawn as a solid block. The first artist had his mind full of the play of curves, which have always meant so much to Celtic artists. The second had had this love of curves swamped by theories of more exact portraiture drawn from the Classical World. On top of that he clearly understood the need for compensating the drawing of his figure, for the view-point of people who were going to look at it. He deliberately drew large and very long faces and a gigantic sword, in order that they should appear in the right proportions when seen at an angle from below. This is something very sophisticated. Our artist probably knew how his fellows in Europe set to work to draw their pictures for mosaic pavements.

Both figures can hardly have been executed in any manner except from an original scale drawing. The hill slope is not steep (12 degrees) and it cannot easily be overlooked from elsewhere. The method of moving men about with marks in their hands, following orders shouted from a distance, which might have been employed at Cerne, Wilmington, or Uffington, may have been used for the goddess, but was not so easy for the other figures. The man who was in charge of cutting the figures, not necessarily the original designer, probably stood on the hillside beside his workmen with a parchment covered with measurements in his hand. This was no work of primitive barbarians hacking a god out of a tree trunk, or like a man cutting a figurehead with an adze. It was an efficient, technical operation, as complicated and as skilled as making a floor picture in mosaic cubes. In neither case can the picture have been executed wholly by eye on the spot. I very much doubt whether the Cerne and Wilmington giants were done without a drawing; although the 'shouted order' method is more possible in their case.

Now the implications here are considerable. We must infer surely a wide degree of education amongst the people who constructed these figures. We are not dealing with naked, blue-painted savages, hiding in swamps, such as have been deduced from the ancient writers. Here we have people who could draw a picture on the equivalent of paper; work out its measurements; write them down in figures; enlarge these to the required size and transfer them to the ground. This is a problem, which would be a strain on the capabilities of many of the products of our modern expensive schools.

It does not follow that the artist could do this. As an artist, his job probably ended with handing in his picture. There was, however, somebody on hand who was completely trained in the mathematics necessary for the execution of the work. This surely gives us a very different picture of conditions of life in Britain, perhaps two thousand years ago, than that to which our early training has led us to expect. It is improbable, for instance, that you would have found the necessary qualifications at the Court of King Alfred nearly a thousand years later. He had the greatest difficulty in getting people trained to read and write.

This was a complete surprise to me. It was a possibility which had never crossed my mind and I should be ready to believe that few, if any, other people had considered it either. I had pictured life at the court of a prince in pre-Roman Britain as something similar to that of the court of Cetzewayo. This picture is evidently completely wrong. It is easy to say that one should have guessed it from the relatively high standard of the coinage of Tasciovanus and Cunobelin; or from the fact that Caesar captured complete muster rolls of defeated Celtic tribes, written in Greek.

Of course Roman writers must have deliberately belittled the good points in the living conditions of their defeated foes and exaggerated such primitive features as they happened to meet. This kind of thing has always tended to falsify the study of history. The winning side tries to gloss over the achievements of the other, for propaganda purposes. So does the loser, if it has a chance. How much truth is there in the stories of terrible atrocities committed by the Vikings? These are all chronicled by the losing side. An occasional cut throat in a drunken brawl, may easily have been reported as the massacre of a whole community. This happened at the time of the revolt of the American Colonies. It happens today in the propaganda of political parties. It is very hard for anyone to contradict once it has been widely spread in print, for, incredible as it may seem, most people believe anything that they can see in writing. There are probably more lies in writing than there are on men's tongues. After all, you can watch somebody who is talking to you, but you cannot see the fellow who is editing a newspaper.

The remarks I have just made about the two male figures, do not apply in the same manner to the goddess. I get the impression, and I know Sir Cyril Fox does the same, that she is made in quite a different style to the others and probably at a different date. I think that perhaps she was designed by eye and by shouting orders for the movement of flags from a neighbouring hill. There is such a hill, marked on the ordnance map, with what is certainly not its original name, as Little Trees Hill. This hill lies west of the goddess and its top is at an angle of about 32 degrees from her central line. If, therefore, you marked out a figure from the hill top, there would be some distortion of the features. In theory, one cannot now see one place from the other because a belt of trees has been planted between the two, the goddess's face, which is an elongated oval on the ground, would have appeared circular from the top of Little Trees Hill. The summit is a few feet above the goddess's head. You would have looked at her at an angle and her legs would not have appeared quite so short as they do on the plan. The distance between the two hills is about the same as that between the hill on which the Cerne giant was cut and the hill facing it. This, I fancy, is what happened at Wandlebury. The goddess's figure was a somewhat primitive Celtic design, worked out by primitive methods, in the centre of a shallow coomb. It is in just such a situation as that in which we find the Long Man of Wilmington and the Uffington White Horse. At one time there was nothing at Wandlebury but a smallish goddess and a peculiar horse. As Sir Cyril and Lady Fox suggested, she was probably Epona, or whatever Epona was called in Britain at that time. Her title was Ma-Gog. At some later date, some changed situation called for the construction of a more developed religious theme and a skilled artist was called in to deal with it. He turned Epona into Artemis and added a moon, a sun god, a chariot and a warrior, all above a white path leading into Wandlebury camp. I think this was all worked out from a picture by measurements.

Epona was a Gaulish horse goddess, said by tradition to have been fathered by a mortal man on a mare goddess. She was in fact a totemistic figure. The addition of the moon symbol turned her into a much greater figure. Epona is probably the Greek goddess 'Hippa', the mother of Apollo, the sun god, and daughter of Pallas and the winged horse. The winged horse is a symbol frequently found on pre-Roman British coins. There was therefore probably little difference in the new meaning of the figure. I shall leave further discussion of this for the moment.

Now, if I have interpreted this correctly, some change had come over the religious or political situation in this part of England to cause the construction of additional figures on a grander scale. It may be of interest therefore to try to sort out what has been learnt about the Iron Age in this district and to see whether it can provide an explanation of the matter.

Since Sir Cyril Fox wrote his *Archaeology of the Cambridge Region* more than thirty years ago, the Iron Age has not received so much attention as some other periods. The picture, however, although very vague, seems to be fairly clear. There were three phases of the Iron Age. I shall not bother the reader with the current archaeological division of the periods into A's and B's and 1, 2 and 3's, for these do not make it any clearer and are somewhat nebulous. There appear to have been three immigrations. The first does not seem to have been a large one and the Iron Age people who came over were relatively simple mixed farmers and herdsmen. They may have reached here about 400 B.C. The second wave is sometimes spoken of as the Marnian Charioteers. They may have arrived two hundred years later. It was this people, a Celtic mixture coming from Gaul, who by intermarriage with the earlier Bronze and Iron Age people living in the district before them, produced the great Celtic tribe of the Iceni. They were a tribe in which rule descended through the female line. This is clear from the story of Boadicea (Boudicca)'s revolt. The Romans violated the queen and her daughters, through whom the royal line descended. Hence the violence of the insurrection and Boadicea's sacrifice of female captives to the goddess Adraste. They occupied the whole of East Anglia and it is fair to assume that Wandlebury was one of their frontier fortresses. A generation before Caesar's conquest of Gaul, a third immigration began into Britain. This was a Belgic, that is a half Celtic and half German people. As far as one can judge, they were far more highly organized than the peoples who had preceded them. Caesar describes them as the

68

most warlike of the Gauls. They seem to have been the first people in eastern England to clear the river valleys and set up stock-raising farms in them.

Archaeology seems to confirm that Wandlebury was in fact a border settlement. There were once two great forts on the spur of hills on which Wandlebury now stands. They are within a mile and a half of each other. One, however, has been completely filled in and will soon have been entirely removed in the quarrying of chalk. This fort, to the north of Wandlebury and overlooking the village of Hinton, which is now known as Cherry Hinton, was accidentally discovered a short while before the Kaiser's war. It was found by quarrymen in a chalk pit and christened the War Ditches by them. The late Professor McKenny Hughes excavated a considerable portion of this earthwork and found many skeletons in the filling of it. I conducted further excavations there in A.D. 1939.[1] Since that time further work has been done, but this remains unpublished. There seems to be little doubt that the fort, a nearly true circle, with entrance on the east, was laid out during the first phase of the Iron Age. But disaster overtook the project and it was never completed. I have found burnt skeletons and charred woodwork thrown into it. There seems little doubt that work was still being carried out when the place was stormed. The workers were killed, the piles of wood for the revetments and stockades burnt and everything tumbled back, still glowing, into the ditch. It was never begun again. By the time of the Roman Conquest it was almost entirely silted up and the filling used for the construction of pottery kilns and burials.

Wandlebury itself, a much greater work of the same type, appears to have been made during the second immigration by the Marnian people. I suppose, it is only a guess, that they were the makers of the Horse Goddess. This seems all the more probable when we regard them as being Iceni. I take this name to have been something like Eachanaidh or Equidios, and to have meant 'The Horse People'.

With the Belgic invasion the area seems to have been occupied by the Catuvellauni, who may have been related to the Chatti from beyond the Rhine. I have found the burial of what I take to be a Catuvellaunian chieftain at Snailwell, thirteen miles

---

[1] *Cambridge Antiquarian Society Proceedings*, vol. XLII.

to the north-east of Wandlebury.[1] He seems to have had a small, light round shield, similar to that shown on one of our figures. Recent excavations, at Peter's Finger in Wiltshire, have demonstrated that Anglo-Saxon shields were often small domed affairs, only twelve to fifteen inches in diameter. Those of the Celto-German Belgae may well have been the same.

It seems probable then that there was a change, at any rate in the political aspect, of this part of Cambridgeshire somewhere about the time of the Birth of Christ. Belgic farmers pressed back the Iceni further into East Anglia. The tribal boundary in this direction was probably the river Lark. There is no reason, however, to suppose that these Belgae did not revere a horse goddess. Their coinage is covered with pictures of horses and some apparently female riders. There are also suns and sickle moons. I feel that it is most likely that our sun god, warrior, chariot and moon were added to the hill by the Catuvellauni somewhere about the Birth of Christ. The Belgic descent was presumably in the male line; therefore they needed a male god, superior in power to the goddess.

However, it is possible that this guess at the dating of the construction of the additional figures at Wandlebury is entirely wrong. From what little I have learnt, in about thirty-five years, of the ancient styles of art in western Europe, there is only one class of objects which seems to bear some resemblance to them. This class is a series of Scandinavian gold pendants known as 'Bracteates'. These were clearly derived in the first place from large Roman gold coins known as 'solidi', dating from about the time of Constantine the Great in the fourth century after Christ. The place of Constantine, however, is soon taken by what is evidently the figure of a deity. In the fifth century the bracteate becomes a thin disc of gold, stamped with the head of this god bearing a very rough resemblance to Constantine. This god is often figured with a horse or perhaps a cow and also swastikas and sun discs. He is evidently a sun god and the whole pendant is a sun disc, or sun amulet. Authorities do not agree over this; but this is my feeling about the objects. They are most commonly found in Sweden and Denmark. Those which reached England in Anglo-Saxon times are of a later and debased type.

[1] *Cambridge Antiquarian Society Proceedings,* vol. XLIII.

Now Gervase of Tilbury mentions the Wandali, or Vandals, in connection with Wandlebury and says that the place took its name from them. This is not believed by students of place names, some of whom prefer to derive the name from the round form of the earthwork. However they need not be right. The earthwork was certainly there before the Emperor Probus transferred Vandals and Burgundians to Britain soon after A.D. 277. Still nobody knows where these Vandals were placed and it is as well to remember that Gervase may have known more about it than students of Anglo-Saxon. The Vandals, in common with the Goths, Suebi and Burgundians, are believed to have crossed from Scandinavia and into east Germany. They are known to history as East Germans. By the time of Probus they had moved westward to the River Maine, almost to the Rhine.

Remembering what Tacitus tells us in his *Germania*, about peoples from this general direction, and then thinking about the bracteates, it seems possible that Vandals might have made figures like those of the sun and warrior at Wandlebury. At the moment I do not think this is the right answer and prefer a Belgic explanation, but I am prepared to learn otherwise. Who, however, is the warrior?

A piece of folk-lore, published in the *Countryman* (vol. liii, No. 1, p. 169), by T. A. Ryder, seems to answer this question. My wife drew my attention to this story. I have heard something like it as a child, but do not ever remember either having heard the giant's name, or having read of him in print. T. A. Ryder's account runs as follows: 'At Horsley, near Stroud, I met an old man who told me this story. The giant WANDIL stole the spring, so winter grew longer and harder till it seemed that the world must die. At last the Gods caught Wandil and made him give up the spring. Like them, he was immortal, but they threw him up into the sky and he became the constellation Gemini. When his eyes (Castor and Pollux) glare down, as on the night of our encounter, there will be a keen frost, and there was. Having heard a similar story from an old Wiltshire shepherd, I looked up the books on legends and folk-lore available to me and could find no reference to Wandil.'

Now Wandlebury has been Wendlesbirri[1] since Saxon times.

[1] Reaney in the *Place Names of Cambridgeshire* derives the tenth-century form, Wendlesbirri, as meaning Waendal's fort.

Our warrior giant has apparently failed in an attempt to arrest the passage of the seasons, that is of the moon. No good interpretation of the place named Wandlebury has yet been offered. It seems hard to believe that our warrior giant is not Wandil. And so we have the names of our three figures still preserved at this place, Gog, Magog and Wandil.

Mr. Ryder suggests that Wandil is connected with the Norse giant, Orwandle, who was worsted by Thor, who threw his toe into the sky to form a star. This may well be so, but the name Wandil is probably older than our Viking wars. Wandil is the age-old demon of winter, dearth and darkness. Castor and Pollux too are traditionally connected with white horses.

The Belgic invasion undoubtedly made considerable changes in the distribution of the earlier Iron Age tribes. When Ptolemy compiled his geography, in the second century after Christ, he located peoples with the same tribal names in different parts of Britain. The pressure of the Belgic tribes seems to have forced numbers of the older peoples to move far north into Scotland and overseas into Ireland. It is clear that this must have taken place, for the Belgic peoples came to occupy nearly the whole of southern Britain from Dorset to Cambridgeshire and large areas elsewhere. Therefore when Ptolemy shows Cornavii on the Welsh Marches and in Sutherland and Dumnonii or Damnonii in Devon and on the Clyde; these distributions do not show the original areas of these tribes; but the areas which they came to occupy as the result of the Belgic pressure. Having been squeezed into smaller areas, parts of the tribes had to migrate. The same thing must have happened to the Iceni. Judging by the place names, their tribal area once extended from Wiltshire to Lincolnshire at Boston. They were, however, squeezed back into Norfolk, Suffolk and Marshland, which at that time stood at least six feet higher above the sea than it does today.

It seemed reasonable to me to look for some settlement of Iceni elsewhere and I have little doubt that they are Ptolemy's Epidii of Kintyre. These are Horse people too. Their modern descendants call themselves MacEacherns, MacEachans or MacEachrans. They claim to have been the great horse people and even that they are descended from a Horse Lord (or Lady?). Having come to this conclusion some years ago, it struck me that if any area could produce further traces of our horse goddess it should be Kintyre. There had been an immigration from Ireland into Argyll in early Christian times; but it was unlikely to have displaced older beliefs. I therefore sent a letter to the *Oban Times* to ask whether any such evidence remained. Little was forthcoming for about nine months, but I then had a most interesting letter from Miss Campbell of Kilberry. Two miles from Kilberry, on the road to Tarbert, the most important portage for boats in the west of Scotland, is a seat of the Cailleach, on to which people must throw a stone to obtain a wish, especially when setting out on a journey. The Cailleach was one of the most important deities in the west of Scotland. Cailleach is not her name, of course, you must not mention that, it just means 'old woman' and has sometimes become rather derogatory. It can be a witch. Nevertheless, the Cailleach was a goddess. Amongst other things she controlled the winds, seas and seasons; she kept a beautiful maiden (Spring or the New Moon?) in a cave in Glencoe, who ran away with Diarmid, the Gaelic Adonis. Numerous rounded hills are named after the Cailleach. They are her breasts. She is the Great Earth Mother in her 'old woman' phase. She is Black Annis of Leicestershire, with her dark face and horrid teeth; but I think she is also the Gruagach, the Fair-Haired One, who is the same goddess in her middle-life phase.

To return to Kintyre, two hundred yards from the Cailleach's seat is 'Slochd na Chapuill', the hollow of the Mare, and just beyond this is 'Glac na h'Imuilte', the hollow of the Struggle. Here, in the hollow of the Struggle, tradition tells of a most peculiar fight. Although it is now spoken of as a Clan battle, nobody knows what clans fought. One of the 'clans' brought a wise woman, a Cailleach, to help them win. The struggle consisted in one side trying to pull the Cailleach off her horse and the other side trying to keep her on it. Now this is most important, for it is clearly an account of an ancient ritual ceremony. The Cailleach is the Earth Mother and a woman riding nude on a horse was widely believed to be a great bringer of Fertility. As I hope we shall see later, the same idea was found in southern Britain. The Cailleach with her horse is the Celtic Artemis, or Diana if you like. She has a dark face in her phase as an old woman and, according to Pliny, the women of Britain used to blacken their nude bodies before attending some of Diana's

Festivals. Black Dianas are known. They are the moon in her dark phase.

So here in Kintyre, just where such a thing had been deduced for entirely different reasons, we have a striking case of the former belief in the great Earth Mother and her magic horse. This to me is one of the most remarkable links in the whole of this unusual investigation. This is just the very place where one might have expected such a thing. Here in the Country of the Horse Folk, is the seat of the Goddess who controls the storms. Without her blessing the seaman could not double the Mull of Kintyre, the Caput Regionis or Epidium of the Romans. Facing the place are the huge mounded breasts of the Earth Mother, the Paps of Jura. To the north are the wild tide rips of the Dorus Mhor and the whirlpool of Corryvreckan where the Cailleach was wont to wash her blanket. If the traveller's stone did not rest on the Cailleach's seat, the oracle showed that there was no prospect of a successful voyage. The goddess who controlled the weather had averted her face. Back the shipmaster must go. There was no safe passage ahead of him, either southward round the Mull or northward to the Firth of Lorne. When once attention is drawn to it, this is the obvious place in which to look; but would one ever think it out without a clue? The clue has come from eastern England.

Chapter Five

(Since various gods and goddesses figure in the text from this
point onwards, it has been thought advisable to summarize
their characteristics in Chapter Ten.)

FOR some hundreds of years these hill-figures have been the
cause of controversy amongst antiquaries. Some were of the
opinion that they dated from Alfred's wars against the Danes;
others ascribed them to the hands of idle monks. Sir Flinders
Petrie in his *Hill Figures of England*, made a gallant attempt to
put them back at least a thousand years before the Birth of
Christ. Although his arguments for this dating are not widely
accepted, he did draw attention to the construction of giant
figures in India and showed possible links with ancient Aryan
invaders, both in the east and in the west. In this I feel that he
was certainly correct. Our hill-figures are not isolated phenomena confined to this island, but are part of a widespread
religious custom. Although only a few remain today, these are
probably no more than the scattered survivors of the more
permanent examples. Many more were probably only drawn,
painted or roughly marked out, for one special day, perhaps not
even once a year. The outlines cut in the chalk downs have taken
the place of effigies designed in a less durable manner.

Sir Flinders Petrie's Indian figure, 'about 60 ft. high is
drawn on the ground, with a white outline, and filled in with
red; the attitude is like that of the Cerne giant, but bears sword
and shield. This represents a demon of darkness, Andhaka, who
is destroyed by Siva in a moonlight festival. As the Indian
demons are the Persian gods, and vice versa, this would accord
with Western Aryans representing deities on a large scale in
this manner.'

This seems to be a most important point to bear in mind
when thinking about our hill-figures. Many a traditional horse

or giant may never have been more than a temporary picture. It is easy to see how the white outlines could have originated, when the simplest way to make a giant figure, on a grassy spot, was to cut turves to form the outline. Year after year the outline deepened and if the subsoil was chalk the hill-figure did not take long to produce. The original idea apparently was not to have a permanent representation of a god or goddess, to be seen year in and year out. It was to make a symbolic figure for one particular occasion, on one particular day or night. The permanent figure is the result of this ceremonial and not the cause of it. In some places the ceremony was fixed to one spot; in others it was processional.

It may seem that I am laying too much stress on this point; but there is a considerable difference between the two ideas. In one case men set out to make the likeness of the particular god whom they intend to worship. In the other they are making a temporary effigy, which may not necessarily represent the god to whom they owe deep respect at all. The picture is what Robert Graves describes as an 'ikon'. The figure may indicate some demon who is to be vanquished by their own god at a traditional ceremony. It is the ceremony which is the important matter and the ceremony has often been remembered longer than the memory of the god in whose honour it was held.

It is interesting to note that, in some folk tales, the Long Man of Wilmington is the effigy of a giant who either killed, or was killed by, another and that the same kind of story centres round Hell Tor on Dartmoor. In each case it seems probable that the ceremony included the killing and destruction of some demon who, like Andhaka of the Indian rite, was supposedly vanquished by one of the people's own gods. At Hell Tor we may perhaps reconstruct the ceremony as ending with the ritual stoning of some figure, painted perhaps on the rock itself. This does not, of course, mean that the figure did not represent a god to some neighbouring people. It is more than likely that it represented the chief god of a hostile tribe. Helith, the Hercules giant of Cerne, could have been worshipped by the Durotriges and reviled by the Dumnonii. Nobody knows whether these two tribes were on terms of friendship with one another or the reverse.

If we return to Geoffrey of Monmouth's story of Goëmagot

and Corineus, we find this kind of situation apparently explained as a result of an invasion of the country by foreigners. Goëmagot is certainly not imaginary, for he was to be seen on Plymouth Hoe only some two hundred years ago. The people of Plymouth paid for him to be re-cut. The invasion may be imaginary. If it is imaginary, then the story can be reduced to the destruction of a club-bearing effigy following a wrestling competition. This may be compared with the horse racing, which accompanied the scouring of the Uffington white horse.

It is at least curious that this Plymouth club-bearer resembles the Helith figure at Cerne. If we are reasoning on the right lines, then he was probably a Helith too and this gives some colour to the idea that Helith figures were unpopular in the West Country. They were, at one time perhaps, gods in Dorset and demons in Devon. There seems little doubt that the Plymouth giant was not regarded as a god by the local people at the time when Geoffrey of Monmouth's Welsh book was written, for he was worsted in a wrestling bout and thrown into the Sound.

In time it should be possible, by the use of archaeology, to show whether Geoffrey's invasion has a solid foundation in fact. At the moment, far too little work has been done for anyone to be in a position to say whether this is so or not. The bulk of archaeological publications gives an appearance of knowledge, which is really only a drop in the ocean of what could be learnt. No one is yet in a position to prove a negative. Judging almost entirely by the topographical distribution of Iron Age camps around Dartmoor, I should guess that some such invasion did take place. But there is no reason to assume either that it resulted in permanent conquest, or that the invaders were not rapidly assimilated into the earlier population. By the time that Geoffrey's Welsh book was written, the popular customs and beliefs may well have reverted to those before any such invasion took place, for a certain and definite conquest by Roman arms had dwarfed any previous tribal struggles. The old festivals and ceremonies emerged from this, much as Guy Fawkes night is still welcomed as a time of rejoicing.

If this is so, then we must doubt the date ascribed to the Cerne figure by Professor Stuart Piggott in his remarkable study of that figure in *Antiquity* (Vol XII). He seems to be

certainly correct in comparing that figure with Hercules, for
the missing lion's skin shows clearly in some air photographs
(Fig. 12). But Hercules was a popular god long before the
Roman Period and a naturalistic figure with a club and cloak
shows plainly on several pre-Roman coins. The Cerne giant,
primitive in some ways and lifelike in others, may be centuries
older than the Roman Conquest of southern Britain. I think

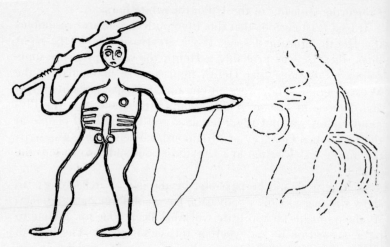

Fig. 12—Sketch composed from the study of several air-photographs
and direct observation of the Cerne Giant. This shows lines which
must almost certainly be a missing cloak and others which may
indicate a second figure. (This is a freehand sketch and not a measured
drawing.)

myself that it was made at least half a century before A.D. 43,
when Claudius began the invasion of Britain. This idea is based
largely on the result of the work done at Wandlebury. It seems
to me that the Wandlebury goddess with her horse, the Cerne
giant and the Long Man of Wilmington are all more or less
contemporary and are certainly older than Roman times. To
these figures one has little doubt in adding the Gogmagog of
Plymouth Hoe, for he is muddled up in an invasion story,
which clearly belongs to a period before the Roman Conquest.

It is now necessary to try to estimate whether there were
once many giants or few. Here there is little to go upon, but

inherent probability. It seems likely that in a primitive land, with comparatively few roadways and of isolated communities, there might have been many places where 'Giant' festivities were observed. There is no need to suppose that these often took place where the figure was displayed on a hillside. Many may have been laid out on the flat. The legend of Hiccafrith suggests that this was so. Few districts in Britain can be found so flat as Marshland around Wisbech; but here is the grave of a giant, who had a wheel for a shield and an axle-tree for a sword. He must surely have been one of the effigies, which we are seeking. Out in that desolate lowland, perhaps two thousand years ago, people seem to have performed a ritual ceremonial combat, similar to the destruction of Andhaka, in India in this present century. There may well have been no permanent figure of Hiccafrith, but the tradition of the ceremony remained down to the present day. His permanent representation was probably the stone known later as his 'candlestick' or 'collar-stud'.

The picture seems to be beginning to make some sense to me. Here and there, all over Britain and probably over Ireland, ritual ceremonies were performed, on some fixed day in the year, in honour of some episode in the mythological story of some long-lost god. These ceremonies were of very great antiquity, perhaps thousands of years old. Here and there the ritual figure, or figures, which formed the central theme of the story were outlined in turf on subsoils, which presently showed through and became permanent outlines. These are but chance survivals from a country-wide galaxy of less permanent figures. They are not necessarily the gods worshipped by the peoples who made them. However, with the movement of populations, they may have come to be worshipped as gods in their own right. From this point it seems possible to start a study of giants and giant stories, from a rational beginning. We are not looking for famous heathen idols, but for fragments of myths. When more than one figure is found, then these are not an ancient pantheon, but probably formed part of a religious drama. Siva destroys Andhaka; some unknown god destroys, or is destroyed by, Helith. Had St. George and the dragon played a part in one of these celebrations, the probability is that only the dragon would have been visible today. It may even be that this is the case. The White Horse of Uffington is viewed from

Fig. 13—The 'Phantom' horse at Bratton, close behind the existing horse. Sketched from an air-photograph published in Marples *White Horses and Other Hill Figures*.

Dragon Hill. The missing horses of Bratton and Tysoe seem to have been remarkable beasts. They may none of them have been horses in the true sense at all.

As I have said before, I do not think that the missing Bratton Horse was ever really destroyed during the construction of the very respectable Georgian beast, which one now sees on the hill near Westbury. If one looks at air photographs of the modern horse, the shadowy figure of the older animal is visible close behind it (*supra*, Fig. 13) and appears very much as if it had once the beaked head of an Iron Age monster.

At Cerne too, it does not seem as if the Hercules figure originally stood alone on the hillside. It is easy enough to imagine that you see things when looking at air photographs, but there do appear to be traces of a figure on the giant's left hand (Fig. 12). There may be nothing there at all and then we are just victims of tricks of light and shade; but the cloak dangling from his extended left arm is clear enough and it surprises me that no attempt has yet been made to expose it. A few hours work, sounding with the bar, would probably show whether there were once companions to this figure. If there were, then I think they have been missing for a very long time and that Helith has survived just because he was a recognizable figure of power and virility. If a group of three or more once existed, they might well go a great way to help us to understand the religious beliefs of people who lived in that district two thousand years ago. Although the labour of looking for them would be great, it might easily be more rewarding than many other forms of archaeological activity.

These gods, beasts, or demons striding on the hills, bring us a picture of ancient ways, which is far more easily appreciated than what we can reconstruct from the scattered traces of everyday life. Pots and pans are pots and pans the whole world over. However, a giant figure, with its ceremonial gathering, the jostling, shouting, dancing and drinking is something much more dramatic.

The little that remains as evidence of the ideas formerly connected with the Cerne giant itself, only serves to show how much has been forgotten. The dancing round the Maypole on the first of May; the barren women creeping up secretly to spend a night on his figure; the boys playing a ritual game beneath his feet, all point to a whole series of former customs and beliefs. What was there originally in that Maypole enclosure above his head? Why has nobody looked to see? Was there never more than a Maypole set there once a year, or did a temple stand inside it, or a sacred grove, or a wooden idol? There may be nothing left to find; but here surely is a place where something of great interest might be discovered. Helith was worshipped, so the thirteenth-century chronicler says (Walter of Coventry: 'in quo pago olim colebantur deus Helith).[1] This seems to imply something continuous and more than just a yearly dance round a Maypole. Maypoles were set up in innumerable villages throughout the country, without anyone recording their connection with a giant.

Perhaps I am wrong, they may have been connected with giants. The reason which makes me wonder may seem very trivial. It is just this: The last Cambridgeshire Maypole used to be raised on Orwell Hill, beside the ancient Mare Way, at its junction with a road which is often assumed to be Roman. Orwell Hill is a high chalk down overlooking the villages of Orwell, Harlton and Eversden. Eversden means 'the boar's wood', if it was originally a Saxon name, or 'boar's hill' if it was Celtic. It seems possible that this name did not refer to some famous wild boar of the wood of that name, but to some effigy of a boar used in a ceremony on the hill. Other Boar's Hills come to one's mind. The Cailleach had her attendant boar, with various places, such as Banavie, named after it.

The Maypole ceremony is usually described as a fertility one. Whether this is truly the case or not, I am not in a position to judge. However, I do know this, when the site of the Maypole ceremony on Orwell Hill was ploughed in 1943, I picked up part of an ancient shell of the large Indian Ocean cowrie (*cyproea panterina*), which is regarded usually as a fertility charm. I have found three specimens of this shell in the graves of women, dating from about the seventh century of our era and also several beads made from the same kind of shell. It seems evident then that things believed to be fertility charms were worn, or

[1] Helith is not peculiar to south-western Britain. Mr. Harold Bayley has reminded me of the barrow with a large boulder on it near Thetford in Suffolk, which is known as the 'Hill of Health'. As recently as 1932, I was told of the local tradition that the Danes had skinned a shepherd on the Hill of Health. The Danes are always blamed for such events in East Anglia. Hiccathrift fought a Dane.

sold, perhaps in the Dark Ages, at the performance on Orwell Hill. I did not find any other objects on the Maypole site, but as I was arranging positions for spigot mortars at the time, this is hardly surprising. It would be more surprising if no objects had ever fallen from the clothing of the Maypole dancers during the many centuries in which this celebration was performed. There must be quite a collection of relics too, trampled into the earth, in the little enclosure above the Cerne giant. Since there can hardly have been a year in which one of the dancers did not shed something, one can make a rough estimate of two thousand objects lying buried beneath the turf. Beads, pins and brooches, coins, buttons and clasps, are all probably represented in that collection.

When archaeologists grow tired of cutting sections through the banks of earthworks, they might well turn their attention to a few Maypole sites. It is quite as interesting to know when and what people introduced the Maypole, as to obtain similar information about earthworks. It would be rather startling if segmented faience beads brought from the Mediterranean, fourteen centuries before the Birth of Christ, were found. Still this might easily prove to be the case. The quest would be quite exciting. After the Georgian coat buttons, Elizabethan earrings, medieval brooches, Saxon beads and Romano-British pins had been collected and labelled, what would come next? Would the series continue back through the Iron Age and into the days of bronze; or would it end suddenly? Nobody knows as yet whether this ancient pagan ceremony was not introduced by the men who built the Megalithic tombs, as far away in time before the Birth of Christ as we are after that event. There would, however, be no great triumphant hole for the director of excavations to show to his admiring visitors. It would be a case of patient slogging away at slowly scraping off the layers of trodden ground.

I suggest this type of research to the keen members of local archaeological societies. No fussy little man can come along and say, 'You are violating a National Antiquity', for there is no National Antiquity to violate. At least one supposes that there is not, but what if there are the post-holes of a wooden temple underneath, or round the edge? Then indeed the investigators would be on the verge of great discoveries and the solution of problems which have baffled all archaeologists. The village

Maypole may have borne the same relationship to more elaborate ceremonies performed in the great stone circles that the
services in the village church bear to those in Westminster
Abbey.[1] Dancing in a circle at a religious ceremony was performed all over the world from the earliest times until the
present day. One has only to watch children playing 'Ring-a-
Roses' to see that they are perpetuating some forgotten religious
ring dance in which some central figure was paid homage. Just
such a scene, as Dr. Margaret Murray observed in her *God of
the Witches*, was depicted on the wall of a cave at Cogul, perhaps
ten thousand years ago.

Sir Flinders Petrie was one of the great men of the last
generation. When therefore he suggests that the Bronze Age
was the probable time in which the custom of making hill-
figures was introduced to Britain, it is not very wise to dismiss
the idea without further thought. It is quite clear that various
new ways of life did come into Britain during the Bronze Age.
People as a whole were changing from herdsmen to mixed
farmers and from stone users to a reliance on metal tools. Trade
goods reached the country from the eastern end of the Mediterranean more than a millennium before the Birth of Christ.
Religious ideas from the south had come in perhaps a thousand
years before that. It is therefore by no means an impossible
suggestion that Petrie made.

The most striking evidence, for the passage of new religious
conceptions from somewhere in the south-east to the north-west
of Europe, is found in Scandinavia. The rock engravings of
Norway and Sweden must be known to most people to-day.[2]
There are very many of these carvings and it has been shown
with some certainty that they were made on sites where religious celebrations were performed. They are believed to range
in time from the end of the Stone Age to as late as the third
century of our era. It is thought that a new picture was made at
each gathering. This seems to be certainly the correct answer,
for there are very many repetitions of the same subject and
pictures have often been placed over earlier ones.

---

[1] Professor V. Gordon Childe has already raised the great stone circles to the
rank of cathedrals. See his *Prehistoric Communities of the British Isles*, p. 102.

[2] A good short account of these carvings and of the problems raised by them can
be found in *Scandinavian Archaeology*, by Shetelig, Falk and Gordon, Oxford 1937.

The most noticeable figures in these collections are those of ships.[1] These are so frequently shown with objects known to be 'sun discs' or sun emblems aboard them, that there is little doubt that they form part of a well-known myth. The sun is carried over his daily path across the heavens in a ship. There are so many representations of sun discs by themselves, men carrying sun discs and so on, that it is clear that sun worship formed a large part of this Bronze Age religion. Other ships, with human figures aboard, are thought to be the 'Boat of the Dead' taking the departed to another world. The cult of the Dead certainly played a large part in Bronze Age religion all over Europe.

When, however, everything connected with ships has been removed from the great collection of pictures, there remain other groupings of figures, which apparently belong to other myths, which have not been yet satisfactorily explained. One group, which occurs on several occasions, represents a male and female figure standing in an amorous embrace, while a third figure armed with axe and sword is advancing towards them. This must represent part of some mythical story, probably of bad behaviour on the part of the northern equivalents of the Olympians Gods (Fig. 14).

There are many pictures of men brandishing spears, which may only represent one figure drawn on many occasions. There are oxen yoked to ploughs, war chariots and wagons, men blowing curved horns and people dancing or walking in procession. These can never be completely identified, but the aim is clear. They are part of a seasonal religious ceremony. In some cases animal figures are thought to represent the beasts offered to special gods at special sacrifices; while the ashes of great fires, below the rocks on which the pictures are engraved, probably indicate the sites of ritual feasts in the Homeric Manner.

Only in the earliest carvings of this series is there any close link with things at present known in Britain. These are representations of the soles of human feet and the cup-shaped hollows, which are so common in Scotland. Both these symbols go back to the Stone Age in Scandinavia. To a rather later period belong pictures of axes, swords, wheels and sun discs. Representations

[1] Tacitus' statement that some of the Suebi worship Isis, whose emblem was in the form of a light war vessel, must be remembered in this connection.

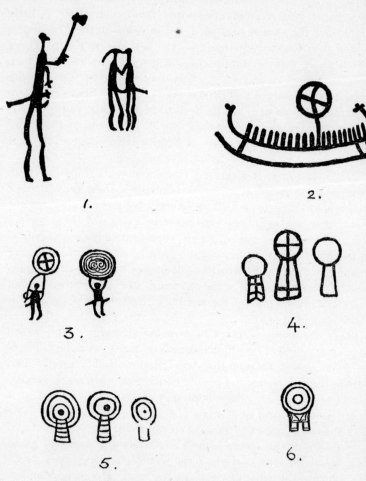

Fig. 14—Scandinavian Bronze Age rock pictures, etc.

1. Mythological scene
2. Moon's ship with Sun's disc   } All from Bohuslan after
3. Men (Priests?) holding up Sun discs }   Bolizer and Norden.
4. The same symbolized

5. Sun symbols of uncertain age from Ilkley, Yorkshire, after Breuil. 6. Sun symbol from 'Pictish' stone. c. A.D. 700.

of axes have only recently been observed on the stones of Stonehenge.

Pictures of human soles, engraved on rocks, are not rare in Scotland, where they are often ascribed to saints or giants. In Scandinavia it has been suggested that they were made to ensure the presence of some god.

The cup markings, which appear to be universal in these Scandinavian sites and which are found occasionally on the walls and even roofs of stone-built graves have long been a problem. The idea that they were libation cups, for offering food to the gods, cannot always be accepted on account of their position. Many, of course, in Scotland were used for the offering of milk to the Little People, until quite recent times and may be still. However the view is now held widely that many more were intended to represent symbols of a goddess and are to be compared with the 'yoni', which in India, together with the phallic 'lingam', forms part of the worship of Siva and his consort Maha-devi. 'Ma' means 'Mother' in every Indo-European language. Maha in India now means great; but this may not have been its original meaning, any more than 'pa' was, which is now applied to the Pope. Maha probably meant 'great Mother.'

If this is the correct explanation, then once again we see a similarity between the religious practices of the Aryan conquerors in India and those of the peoples who migrated westwards into north-western Europe. It is not the only kind of similarity that has been observed. Many readers will remember that 'dolmen' tombs of Iron Age India are paralleled by similar tombs in the west, constructed with a difference in time of perhaps two thousand years. There was apparently some unknown centre from which waves of ideas were carried both westward and south-eastward at differing times. One wave seems to have reached Britain and Scandinavia towards the end of the Stone Age; not necessarily by the same route as others reached those areas, in the Bronze Age. The Stone Age wave, the Megalithic Men, appears to have come by the long sea route up the Atlantic coasts of Europe, while the others trekked overland. The peoples too were of very different racial types. One might almost feel that the Megalithic wave corrsponded to the Dravidian, pre-Aryan, population of India and that the remaining waves were Aryan.

It seems probable that everywhere the later waves absorbed some of the beliefs and rites of the earlier ones. The lingam and yoni emblems do not appear to have belonged to the religion of the Aryan invaders of India; neither do the cup hollows appear to have been introduced by the Bronze Age peoples into Scandinavia. In both cases they were there already. Still, although from very early times men depicted animals and boats on rocks in Norway, presumably as a kind of magic to aid them in their hunting, yet the particular type of rock engraving we are considering, with its indication of religious myth and rite, does not appear before the full Bronze Age. It looks therefore as if this general type of representation can be expected from Aryan immigrants of the Bronze Age. So far there is no archaeological flaw in Petrie's theory.

Of course no one knows exactly who, or what, Aryans are or were. The term has no real racial value. However there still remains a kind of basic language, which may be called Aryan, or Indo-European, and it looks as if there was also a sort of collection of religious beliefs, which might be described by the same name. Neither religion, nor language, is necessarily any indication of race. The Aryan family of peoples is still wrongly connected in men's minds with the term 'Nordic', which is under a cloud owing to the unfortunate behaviour of Adolph Hitler. The difficulty is that few anthropologists can agree as to what consitutes a race, or even whether there is such a thing at all. This is all part of the progress of science, but it can scarcely be called helpful.

The chief reason for doubting Petrie's dating of our hill-figures is that they do not appear to conform to the art forms of that period; while points of resemblance have been noted between one of them and certain figures of our early Iron Age. I do not know who first made the suggestion; but people had been talking of it long before it appeared in print. The Uffington White Horse certainly has the appearance of being an Iron Age animal and it is hard to believe that it was made at any time before perhaps 200 B.C. But it is necessary to remember that this opinion is based on what has been learnt from the study of the art forms found on small ornaments. While the date of these is known with some certainty, no one can really say whether it had not originated on much larger things, such as carved door-posts, or even great wooden idols resembling the totem poles of North America. It is quite possible that our hill-figures were traditional forms, the idea of which had been carried right across Europe and only became fixed to one spot when they reached Britain. We only know of the Indian Andhaka figure because of the custom of making him which has persisted down to the present century. Had our hill-figures originated in the same way, as I think they did, then there may well have been innumerable ancestral effigies of the Cerne Helith, or the Uffington Horse, made at the halting places of migrating tribes, year by year, between the shores of the Black Sea and England. They would presumably have been made in one traditional style; just as Andhaka was depicted, in the days of high explosives, with a sword and shield.

Now, the discovery of the Wandlebury figures has doubled the material available for present study. Where formerly we had the Long Man of Wilmington, Helith of Cerne and the Uffington White Horse, there are now three more. One of these appears to be a sun god completely different from any known Iron or Bronze Age object. The other two, however, have features in common with the original specimens. Both the chariot goddess and probably the figure with the sword have eyes formed, like spectacles, in the same primitive manner as the Cerne Giant. The goddess's draught animal, whether it be a horse or not, has curious disconnected outlines similar to the Uffington beast. It seems then that these five figures, the Cerne giant, the Wandlebury sword-bearer, the giantess, her horse and the Uffington horse, all belong to one family. It is only reasonable to suppose that they belong to roughly the same date. This in itself is helpful, but there is more to it than that. While the Uffington horse was probably made in the Early Iron Age, the Wandlebury beast almost certainly was. It has a most peculiar beaked nose. This nose is characteristic of the so-called 'Celtic' art and representations of it have been found in many parts of Europe as well as Britain. The closest resemblance I have been able to find to it is a figure on a finger-ring from Filottrano in Northern Italy, which is dated by Professor P. Jacobsthal to about 400 B.C. There are, however, many pictures of similar noses on objects found in Britain of dates believed to be almost as late as the Roman Conquest.

We can now perhaps feel a little more confident. These figures all belong to one group and the date of that group is almost certainly somewhere between 400 B.C. and A.D. 43. There is no direct way of narrowing the dating, but of the three sites where these figures figures occur, two are close to large Iron Age camps. It is hard to believe that they had no connection with these camps, for in each case the camp was associated with ceremonies. The probability is that the owners of these forts made the figures. The chief occupation of the Wandlebury earthwork seems to have been in the second phase of the Iron Age and it is probably reasonable to pick on the year 200 B.C. as the approximate time for the cutting of the goddess figure. This may be many years out, but it conforms to the rules of Inherent Probability.

Chapter Six

NOW comes the time when it is necessary to make an attempt to deduce who these figures were meant to represent. I do not think that there is any one answer to this question. It seems that in the Celtic world, as in the Roman Empire and in ancient Greece or India, there was a tendency for local gods to coalesce and for myths, belonging originally to several different religions, to be joined into one worship. The process continued into Christian times and we find ancient Celtic gods and goddesses becoming saints. A typical example is Brigid, the Celtic goddess of fire and fertility.

Our figures will therefore probably show features belonging to more than one religious conception. We can, however, I think, reconstruct the myth which the ceremony was meant to reproduce. If we can accept Gervase's original story, then this was a moonlight festival. The figures appear to show a goddess, with a waning moon above her head, walking her tired horse up a ribbon of white. Behind her a figure waves a sword, but he seems to have been unable to stop her passage and has perhaps been wounded in the attempt. Before the goddess a huge round figure appears above her on the hillside, with rays streaming from his head. He must be the rising sun.

This is surely a remarkable coincidence, for is not this the same story as that of Siva destroying Andhaka in a moonlight festival? The third figure, with his sword and shield, must be the demon of darkness, who has tried to stop the moonlight and been worsted by the sun. If this is right, then the goddess is the Celtic equivalent of Maha-devi, Siva's wife. We have already seen both of them deduced by scholars from rock engravings in Scandinavia.

Had I not spent a lot of time poring over a book, which is

not, I am sure, considered orthodox reading for an archaeologist, namely Harold Bayley's *Archaic England*, I should have stuck at this point. However, he has no hesitation in lumping the Meg and Mag names of stone circles, together with Magog and explaining her as the Great Mother, the Great Earth Goddess and a source of fertility.

Once again the coincidence is too great. There are four Meg's or Mag's hills, each of them rounded, breast-like hills, within four miles of our goddess. The hills on which she lies are the Gogmagog Hills and she apparently has four breasts in the picture. She must be Magog. Just as Magog's name seems to have been applied to these breast-shaped hills here; so was that of the Cailleach, a female deity, in western Scotland. There are two, close together, on either side of Broadford in Skye. They are the breasts of the Great Mother. At the same time, or so it seems to me, she must be Maha, Siva's wife and the sun god must be Gog. Of course, his Celtic name may have been Belenus, or Taranis, and she would certainly have been Diana in Roman times. But the local aboriginal inhabitants, overrun in turn by Celts, Belgae, Romans, Saxons, Norsemen and Normans, knew them by the ancient root-names, common over wide areas of the earth, as Gog and Ma-Gog. As late as the eleventh century of our era, Canute had to stop the worship of the sun and moon.

Gog is the sun, the rolling, goggling, all-seeing eye, just as Siva is the shining one. Ma Gog is the moon, under whose pale light the love-making took place and the children were born. The victory of these two light bringers over the power of darkness is what I think these figures symbolized. Did not Gervase describe the mysterious enemy as being all in black with a black horse? Actually the figure must have been white, but it may have been darkened for the ceremony, or reddened like Andhaka.

Strangely enough the Helith figure at Cerne appears to be Gog too. He is Helith, synonym for Hercules; but Hercules is also Ogmius in Roman Gaul. If he is traced a little further afield, the Baal of Hiram, king of Tyre, was represented as Hercules. But Baal was a sun god and his Beltane ceremonies survived in Britain down to the eighteenth century. A doggerel rhyme names the Cerne Hercules as Beelzebub.

Gog and Magog seem to have been the Powers of Light, but

somehow at Plymouth their combined names appear to have
been transferred to a giant who was worsted and thrown over a
cliff. There are suggestions that there was once a second figure
there. Were there not three? Did not Magog and the demon
drop out of the story and the single Gogmagog remain? The
story told by Geoffrey of Monmouth of the unfortunate end of
Gogmagog makes this the consequence of a foreign invasion.

Has not the same thing happened at Cerne? The Cerne
Hercules was Helith and Hercules was the sun god. His name
must surely be related to the Greek Helios, the sun. The Maypole dance above his head was a sun disc festival and it was held
on Beltane, the day of Baal's fires. So it is with Hell Tor, which
can never have been the dark, or shady tor, for it must always
have stood above the heavy tree line. If there are other figures
at Cerne, then, on this hypothesis, they will be Magog and the
Demon. Whether I am right or wrong, their discovery would
be of very great interest.

Then there is Hiccafrith. It is not clear from the traditions
whether Hiccafrith was the name of the warrior armed with the
wheel and axle-tree, or of his adversary. But it does seem most
likely that here was performed a repetition of the same rite.
The figure with the wheel sounds once again as if he were the
sun figure, a Celtic sun god with the wheel symbol. His name
has gone; he was merely described by the Saxons as the Trust
of the Iceni.

Testimony to the former power of these long-lost gods still
remains with us in the names of the first two days of the week.
Why were they not ousted by other gods in the northern pantheon, such as Thor, Woden and Frey, if they were not still
regarded as very powerful in popular belief? Can it have been
that the Romano-British part of the population, and London in
particular, claimed their share of the days of the week? It may
well be so. London paid great veneration to Gog and Magog.
How Magog came to change her sex, we shall never know.

We seem to have stumbled on widespread evidence of the
former worship of the powers of Light and the mythological
representation of their war against the powers of Darkness.
With the powers of light are also associated the emblems of
fertility. Magog is the Great Mother, the Earth Goddess;
together with the sun she renewed the seasons and dispelled

the winter darkness. The most widespread ceremony, formerly performed throughout the land at the beginning of summer, was the setting up of the Maypole on the first of May. The Maypole was crowned frequently with a wheel, the symbol of the sun, of Jupiter, or Belenus, or whatever the chief god happened to be called. Here then are two symbols of sun worship associated together at a ritual dance. There is the pole, which is thought to be a fertility symbol and the wheel, which is certainly a sun symbol. The Maypole was always set up in the enclosure above the Cerne Giant. But the wheel and pole were the emblems of Helith. If Helith is Hercules, he has the right to Jupiter's wheel. This must have belonged to Gog also. And so it appears that the Maypole ceremony at Cerne belonged originally to the surviving giant. The Gaulish Hercules was known as Ogmius, which appears to be a variant of Gog. The Irish knew him as Ogma Sun-face and also Balor.

Whatever may be the true explanation of the problem, it is clearly important to try to show whether, or not, there are other figures beside the giant of Cerne. If he stands alone on that hill, then he represents a version of the sun, which is to be expected. Helith also may easily be a Celtic variant of Helios, the sun. The 'Heel' stone at Stonehenge fits somewhere into this picture. In this case one of the Plymouth figures should have been Gog also. Perhaps it might still be possible to recover them. I have not been to look.

The Long Man of Wilmington is known to have been restored. It is by no means certain that all his details have been preserved or that those which we now see are original. The elaborate calculations made by Petrie do not appear to lead to any definite conclusion as to whether the rising of the sun played any part in orientation of this figure. However, Petrie does draw attention to the idea that the Long Man was represented as opening the Doors of Heaven and that his position, facing north, would be in keeping with that of the eastern god, Varuna. This seems to fall in with the results already deduced from this study. Eastern myths have travelled across Europe and lodged in Britain. However, the Long Man may not belong to the Gog and Magog myth. Perhaps he is part of something else. More could be learnt about him by careful examination. There is no clue as to whether he has always been alone on the hillside and nothing very much can be deduced from the traditions which clung to him; except that he, or some other figure, was probably subjected to the stoning ritual. Is he opening the doors of Heaven, or is he holding up two sun discs on poles, in the manner shown on some of the Scandinavian rock carvings? It is impossible to say without an examination. He may be a sun figure, but he is not a Hercules. It seems most unlikely that he belongs to any period than that of the others. An examination might show that he has the same spectacle eyes. The idea that he was made by idle monks appears quite absurd. Nothing but strong religious feeling could account for the labour entailed in cutting him out. He must be left in peace for the moment, with the feeling that he too may be something to do with some sun myth and that he could be opening the Doors of Heaven after a triumph over the demon of darkness.

The horses, for it is, I think, clear that there were at least three ancient ones, Bratton, Uffington and Tysoe, appear at first sight to belong to some entirely different ritual. This is not necessarily the case. Dr. Margaret Murray has drawn attention to the story of Lady Godiva and the probable connection between her white horse and the White Horse of Uffington. Mr. Harold Bayley has suggested that the Uffa of Uffington is not derived from some unknown Anglo-Saxon landowner, but related to the Greek Ippos, a horse. Ippos itself is clearly related to the name of the north Gaulish horse goddess, Epona. It might seem from this therefore that our three ancient horses were mere symbols of Epona and that Lady Godiva was just taking the place of the goddess at some ritual procession at Coventry in honour of Epona.

The story of the wicked earl who made his virtuous wife ride naked through the town before he would ease his demands on its inhabitants may well have some foundation in fact. She was made to take the place of the girl who would normally have ridden in the procession. However, I suspect that, though the countess's baptismal name was Godiva (she was certainly a real person), this was also the name by which any rider in the procession was known. I think it was a local Latin title for the goddess she represented. It was Gog-diva, the holy lady Gog. In other words the rider represented Ma Gog. The procession represented both the passage of the moon across the night sky and the change from winter to spring. The wicked earl may be no more than our old friend, Wandil or Andhaka, while the lady is the same personage as the one we have seen toiling up the hillside at Wandlebury. Two stories may easily have been confused. The countess may never have been involved in this procession.

There is no tradition of a procession at Uffington, but there were horse races, a fair and general jollity. At Tysoe nothing survived but the jollity. However, this was regarded as so important in the village, that when the original horse was destroyed another was made to replace it. And what happened at Banbury Cross? Who was the fine lady who rode on a white horse? Was she not Godiva, who in a similar ceremony at Southam, between Coventry and Banbury, was painted black? I suspect that the Coventry ritual was once also practised at Tysoe, which is only twenty miles distant, and also at Banbury. Although the Tysoe horse was on red soil, it could easily have been whitened for the occasion. These ritual processions of nude women on white horses, riding out to confer benefits on the people, are closely related to the Kintyre tradition. There the struggle with the demon of darkness was actually prortayed in mimic conflict. Godiva at Coventry was veiled in her hair; at Southam she was painted black. The ceremony would have ended in an unveiling, when the New Moon was then revealed. At Banbury she had bells on her toes to scare off the demon. Demons hate noise. That is what the bells are for.

The whole of Britain is full of traces of white horses. Sometimes, as at Finchampstead, Berkshire, they have become ghost horses. At other times you find them on whisky bottles or traction engines. The horseshoe has become a lucky talisman; but it was once a lunar symbol and a fertility charm. The horse was sacred to Diana because of its moon-shaped hoof. We get here into such a maze of odd scraps of information that it would take many pages to try to sort them out. We have Tacitus's description of the sacred white horses of the Germans, which were used like the Cailleach as oracles, and we have the white-horse banner of Wessex. Horses, no doubt these sacred horses, are found drawn on Iron Age pots in Gaul and I have found them scratched on Anglo-Saxon burial urns in Suffolk. They occur on Iron Age ornaments on the Continent and on Romano-

British brooches in Britain. You find the ancient 'Horse-People' tribe of the Epidii in Kintyre about A.D. 100 and at the same time the Iceni, who must surely be the Each, or horse-people in Norfolk and Suffolk. You find the horse on numberless pre-Roman British coins.

To this day you may see the brass symbols of a horse's head, or a horse's shoe, dangling on the chest of a cart horse. I think these are all relics of one worship. Epona, Diana, Magog, or Maha-devi are all names for the same goddess and she is the Moon or Earth Mother. She may be young as Epona; in middle life like Diana; or old like the Highland Cailleach. These are just phases of the moon. The Cailleach, the Gruagach and Black Annis are probably one and the same goddess. They are Magog in her capacity of Kali the Terrible, who is also Maha-devi. The Gruagach had cup-marked stones named after her in the Highlands.

Why do the Continental representations of Epona show her with a key in her hand? This is usually explained as being the key of the stables; but men do not pay great reverence to a goddess whose only power is to be able to unlock the stable door, or ease the glanders, they want something for themselves Epona is holding the Key of Heaven, just as the Long Man of Wilmington appears to be opening the doors.

Looking at the question as impartially as may be, which is the more probable? Is it more likely that all these things are just a collection of coincidences; or are they evidence of the former existence of a very widespread creed and ritual? To me there seem to be far too many coincidences. Whatever line of approach you take, you seem to end up at the same point. You appear to come up against traces of a belief, underlying all the little creeds of different tribal godlings, that the powers of light, typified by the sun and moon, waged a perpetual war against the powers of darkness. It was to aid the powers of light in their struggle, to assist the powers of productiveness if you like, that people re-enacted these myths, year by year. When the sun and moon came back again in power, in answer to these ceremonies, everyone rejoiced.

This must have been a creed which originated in a relatively high latitude. It cannot have been thought out in India or Egypt, but in some land where winter and summer were clearly divided. It must have spread in many directions from some common centre where men had time to think things out. Somewhere, at least four thousand years ago, men evolved a belief, which seemed so obviously correct at the time that it was accepted wherever it was carried. Its spread must have been one of the great events in the history of the world. It took untold centuries for it to break up into little local creeds and these tended to coalesce once more. Quite a lot of it remained at the back of medieval Christianity, and may almost be said to be the underlying principle of modern civilization. Gog and Magog may have gone from our daily lives, but the ideas which brought them into being remain. Light and darkness must always be at war.

There is one more aspect of this problem, which I shall be rash enough to mention. Siva, in one of his aspects, is the destroyer of life: Maha-devi, in her Kali aspect, is also a destroyer. Yet at the same time they are worshipped as the bringers of fertility. This is explained by the belief of their devotees in the transmigration of souls. Transmigration is not quite the same as reincarnation, for it includes the belief in man's rebirth as a lower animal. This belief is presumably the result of the mingling of the reincarnation belief with totemism. Death is just the gate to another bodily existence. But the one thing which made a great impression on many Roman writers, including Julius Caesar, was that the Druids believed also in the transmigration of souls. Various attempts were made by Classical authors to explain how this belief had reached the Gauls. Some maintained that it had been taught them by a supposed disciple of Pythagoras, others that it was through contact with Brahminism. Sir Thomas Kendrick in his book on the Druids[1] gives all the known passages. He formed the opinion that this belief, being found today among primitive peoples, necessarily evolved among them. But this need not be the case. It may have spread to them. It looks to me very much as if the transmigration belief is part and parcel of the other and that the Druids were, in fact, the priests of Gog and Magog. Just as with the Brahmins, a host of other gods and godlings became associated through the ages into a polytheistic pantheon, so did the original great Celtic luminaries become obscured in a multitude of other

[1] Sir Thomas Kendrick, *The Druids*, Methuen 1927.

deities. However, Britain was said to be the land in which Druidism was to be found in its purest form. It seems likely that had the mass of verses, which the Druids were compelled to learn by heart, been committed to writing, they would have shown many resemblances to the Hindu writings.

The other and most shocking thing about Druidism was its method of Human sacrifice. This the Romans put down with the utmost rigour. Their method of sacrifice was to enclose felons and captives in huge wicker cages made in human form, and then burn them alive. Many people have called attention to the resemblance between these wicker cages and the former processional figures of Gog and Magog in London. Sir Thomas Kendrick, however, supplies the clue to what these sacrificial figures were really. He found that in France, till recent times animals were burnt in wicker cages to ensure a good yield of crops. They were, in fact, sacrificed to promote fertility.

This appears to explain the Druidical custom. Felons and people hostile to the public good represented the forces of Darkness. They were enclosed therefore in an effigy of the demon of darkness and destroyed for the pleasure of Gog and Magog and to ensure fertility to the people and country-side. This was not just a piece of beastly cruelty, but a very serious and important religious rite. The priests did not meet together and say, 'It's time we had a jolly holocaust, boys.' They thought that they had discovered, by their astrological reckoning that a great sacrifice was necessary to prevent a famine, or some other national disaster.

Thus the Druids seem to fall naturally into place in this picture. They venerated Jupiter's oak; they cut the sacred mistletoe from it with a moon-shaped knife, and they constructed and destroyed effigies representing the powers of darkness. That is almost the sum of all the knowledge that we have about their actions. However they did profess the same doctrine of the transmigration of souls, which is the chief tenet of the Brahmins, many of whose other customs seem to resemble closely those of Celtic Britain.

In putting forward the theory that Druidism and Brahminism had a common origin, in an unknown area, at a very distant time, I am only collecting and sorting out small pieces of information. When I began the process, I had not the slightest idea whether any picture could be formed from these pieces; nor the faintest glimmer of thought as to what form it might take. The picture has formed like a jigsaw puzzle and each piece I take up appears to fit into the same picture. To begin with I thought that I had stumbled on a series of pictures of isolated Celtic gods at Wandlebury and that these were actual idols to be worshipped as such. It was only later, when Sir Cyril Fox suggested it to me, that I began to look at the figures as a group intended to tell some actual story to those who saw them. Then, going back to Sir Flinders Petrie's notes in his *Hill Figures*, the similarity between our figures and those in India impressed itself on me and I began to sort out all the information, which I had collected while attempting to identify the single figures of gods. The surprise with which I watched the picture grow exceeded that which I experienced when each Wandlebury figure began to form on paper.

The question of where this religious theory of the struggle between the powers of light and darkness was evolved is very difficult. From its very antiquity it is improbable that an exact answer can be found. However, there are some clues. The first I have already mentioned. The religion was bound up with the importance of the seasonal change from summer to winter. It could not have been evolved in hot climates with little obvious change in temperature. Furthermore, it appears to have spread outwards as far as Britain, Syria, Greece, Italy and India from a common centre. Faint waves of thought from it even reached the Aborigines of Australia and probably went all round the world. It was a better idea than that of totemism, which preceded it; but the two ideas became mixed and resulted in polytheism in many lands.

Druidism is regarded as essentially a religion of the Celts, but I am not sure that this is the correct answer. It appears to be older than the authentic Celtic migrations. Still, here we are muddled by this vexed problem of race. By the time the Celts reached western Europe, they must have been of very mixed blood. Words of many different languages would have been babbled by half-caste children as they played round the wheels of the wagons in a Celtic laager. The warrior class may have remained relatively unmixed, as the Aryans attempted to do in India; but the Celts had not the rigid morality, which Tacitus ascribes to the Germans, and little bastards must have been more common than the pure-blooded children. There is no clear way of telling whether the Celts originated the belief, or whether they picked it up somewhere on their travels and accepted it. There is no means of telling either if the Bronze Age peoples in Scandinavia, who seem to have held to this faith, were of what might be called Celtic stock or not. They may well have been a wave of peoples who at a later time would have been called Keltoi in Greece, or Gauls in France.

However, it seems that the burial rite of cremation is also mixed up in this story. Although this was not probably included in the earliest ritual; it appears to have been closely associated with all the later stages of it. Dr. Margaret Murray's extensive studies on the religion of the witches in western Europe, a cult which had some of the features of the Gog and Magog worship, show that its devotees insisted when possible on being burnt. This particular faith can hardly have been a survival of Druidism in its more developed form; but, with its insistence on fertility rites and dancing in a ring, it may be a relic of that religion in its earlier stage.

The rite of cremation was widely practised in the Bronze Age and was also customary with many of our early Iron Age tribes. It seems to have been the orthodox way of releasing the dead person's spirit from the necessity of hanging about round its recent home. The soul was, in fact, being set free for its transmigration. It is being sent to Gog or Siva for its new posting. That is why the Druids burnt their captives. They were being sent directly to the God for transference into some unpleasant future existence as a slug, or a bed-bug. Should you only cut their throats and leave them lying about, their earthbound spirits would haunt the place and be a menace.

If therefore we could find the area in which cremation was first practised, it might be a pointer to the birth-place of the religion. This is not easy to do and I shall not attempt to do so; but it is at once clear that archaeologists do not see the earliest known ancestors of the people, later known as Gauls or Celts, as being adherents of the rite of cremation.[1] These early, or proto-Celts are visualized as coming from the area which extends from Central France to Bohemia. Some authorities hold

[1] Cf. J. M. de Navarro, *The Cambridge Ancient History*, vol. vii, pp. 54 et seq.

that the western boundary should be on the Rhine. This people, known as Zoned-Beaker people, inhumed their dead and continued to do so throughout the Bronze Age. These Zoned-Beaker people were apparently conquered at the end of the Bronze Age by an Alpine tribe who practised cremation. The absorption of this second people, the Urnfield men, into the proto-Celts is suggested as being the origin of the true Celts. Here at once one sees the idea of a pure Celtic race destroyed. There was no such thing. Even if there is doubt as to the exact composition and distribution of the early Celts; it does not seem probable that they were the originators of the idea of the cremation rite, or of the worship of Gog and Magog. These were beliefs which they had accepted somewhere on their travels.

Were these ideas originated then by the Urnfield Culture, or did they spring from somewhere further to the east or north? Could they perhaps have come from somewhere in Asia Minor? Here we must be struck once more by the mention in Ezekiel of both Gog and the land of Magog. Where was this land and was it the original home of Magog? It seems fairly clear that Magog's land was that of Meshech and Tubal, of which Gog is the chief prince. Tubal or Tabal is thought to be a small area north of Syria in Asia Minor It is enclosed by the Taurus Mountains to the south and the Anti-Taurus to the north-west. Gomer, which is also mentioned, lies to the north-east of Tubal. From very early times Sun worship was widespread in this part of the world and south-eastward into Mesopotamia. Many religions, including that of Mithras, have originated in these areas and in the valleys of Persia. Whilst, however, many waves of northern tribes appear to have pushed south-eastward across the Bosphorous and into the mountain masses beyond, I cannot think of any historic movements in the opposite direction. Cimmerians, who are often thought to have been Cymbri from Denmark, have ended up on the head-waters of the Tigris. Galatae, who were certainly Celts, ended their days of independence in Asia Minor. The Hatti, or Hittites, are thought to have spoken Celtic. It seems probable that the Aryan invaders of India were one of these northern waves driving south-eastward. There is less certainty that some movements from Asia pushed up into north-western Europe.

The social organization of the Aryans in India appears to

resemble that of the Celts more closely than it does the Teutonic, or Nordic, if that term is preferred, system. Although Tacitus describes priests among the German tribes near the Rhine; when we see the northern peoples in the Viking Age, the priest and chieftain are often the same person. Among the Celts, the Druids had become a highly organized priestly caste, which took no other part in the social organization. Amongst the Brahmins, the same situation still exists.

It is true that Tacitus mentions a priest when he describes the various tribes around the modern Denmark as worshipping Nerthus, or Mother Earth. In her shrine in a sacred grove on an island in the sea was a draped car, in which the priest could feel the goddess when she chose to come. Then her car was drawn by cattle throughout the land of the Reudigni, Aviones, Anglii, Varini, Eudoses, Suarini, and Nuitones. Wherever the Goddess was taken, men locked away their weapons and all iron was concealed. People gave themselves to peace, rejoicing and merrymaking till Nerthus was taken back to her isolated home. Then the goddess, car and covering were all washed in a secret lake by slaves, who were at once drowned so that they should not talk of what they had seen. Two at least of these tribes, the Anglii and the Eudoses, later became part of the Anglo-Saxon people.

If this is a relic of the worship of Magog, it is curious that the slaves were drowned and not burnt. It may well have been once part of the same ritual; but have decayed through time and isolation, or it may have been an earlier stage in the religion.

The Suevi, beyond these tribes, were known by Tacitus to have worshipped Isis, with a war galley as her symbol. He tells us that he could not understand how this foreign religion had reached them. But we know a little more today, for the war galley was certainly the ship of the Scandinavian rock engravings and reached the north hundreds of years before the days of Tacitus. Isis was a moon goddess and also a goddess who protected shipping. The shape of a ship recalled the shape of a sickle moon; just as the shape of a horse's hoof suggested the moon to the votaries of Diana. However the ships are frequently drawn with sun discs in them and so you have both sun and moon symbols in the same picture. As far as one can see, however, there is no demon of darkness. The sun and moon are there, but the myth is incomplete.

Perhaps this is incorrect. The male figure with raised axe, who is frequently shown advancing to attack a loving couple, may be the enemy trying to catch the sun and moon unawares (Fig. 14).

Therefore it looks as if this religion had reached and been accepted in Scandinavia at an early stage, before the priesthood had developed into a caste of Druids. I have suggested in another book, *Boats and Boatmen*, that the particular type of boat shown on the rock engravings probably reached Scandinavia from somewhere in south-eastern Europe in the Early Bronze Age. The appearance of this sun and moon religion may well point in the same direction. If that is so, it looks like evidence for a migration from the south-east to the north-west in the opposite direction to the general run of such movements in historic times. But this may have happened and it is quite likely that it did. Objects and ideas certainly travelled from south to north. The climate of the earlier part and much of the full Bronze Age, is known to have been warmer and drier than it is to-day. Areas to the south-east may have become unbearably hot and dry, while good farming and grazing lands could be colonized further north. Later in the Bronze Age we know that the climate deteriorated and it is then that we begin to hear of fierce northern tribes forcing their way southwards. They had to do this or starve. Their fields were becoming waterlogged, their sheep were getting liver fluke, their grain would not ripen and their hay would not dry. There was nothing for it but to fight their way south. Once begun, the movement was hard to halt. Begun perhaps by a few farmers around Trondheim, it would go on gathering younger sons and landless men all the way across Europe, till the wave burst with a crash on the old civilizations of the south.

The late Sir William Ridgeway was clearly right when he said, in his *Early Age of Greece*, that the culture of the Acheans in the Homeric poems showed that they were a northern people who had settled amongst Mediterranean tribes. However, it seems that the Achean invasion of Greece must have taken place long before the climatic deterioration in the north and that some other cause forced this people to leave their original homes.

It is not impossible that in the warmer summers of the Bronze Age there was considerable melting of the Polar Ice Caps and that there is much truth in the story told by the Druids of movements southward of their ancestors due to the flooding of their homelands. From my own observations I know that former Bronze Age land surfaces are now beneath the sea at high water in many places round the west of Scotland. Similar observations have been made all round our coast and that of north-west Europe. Many fertile lands of the Bronze Age are now beneath the North Sea. The flooding process continued right into the Middle Ages and is now becoming apparent once more.

At the beginning of this Bronze Age, perhaps about 1800 B.C., the British Isles became dominated by a race who we know as the Beaker people. In spite of suggestions by various authorities to the contrary, it seems probable that this was a relatively numerous people who did more than form a small ruling caste over the Neolithic, Megalithic and other peoples, who were already in Britain before them. Their earlier burials are usually found as crouched skeletons and it is not till later that cremation becomes a universal rite in the land. As far as I know, all our larger circles on the mainland and in Ireland which have been excavated, suggest, whether they are built of stone or show sockets for wooden posts, that the Beaker people were the first to use them. This is important, for many of the Scottish circles are associated with the cup markings which we have reason to believe were symbols of Magog. The circles themselves could well be sun discs. In fact it looks very much as if the Beaker people introduced an early form of the worship of Gog and Magog.

Now this Beaker people was related by culture, if not by blood, to the Zoned Beaker–Proto-Celts of the Continent. They were a broad-headed, strongly built race to whom an Alpine ancestry is usually ascribed. To them, in a later phase of the Bronze Age, was added an offshoot from the Urnfield people. Unfortunately the rite of cremation has destroyed the possibility of judging anything about their physical appearance. It is clear, however, that by Anglo-Saxon times and probably before that, the Beaker man's physical type had been largely bred out. You do see specimens of people of the Beaker type in Britain to-day; but, in the excavation of several hundreds of Romano-

British and Anglo-Saxon graves, I have never found a single example; although I have found several in Beaker Period burials in East Anglia. The reason why the Beaker type had vanished from the east of England is not known. It may have been economic; or it may have been genetic. Since, however, the Beaker people's economy was largely pastoral and apparently migratory, they would have tended to become squeezed out when agriculture developed. The reason that Beaker types are not found in later times in the east of England may only be that there was no room for their accepted way of life and they moved over to the moorlands of the west and north. Here they can still be observed, especially in the hills.

On the other hand, it is perhaps more probable that the broad-headed strain cannot stand up against others in breeding. Our medieval graveyards contain numerous broad-headed skulls, which probably reflect the long connection between England and France in the Middle Ages. There is no such large proportion of broad heads to-day. It has been largely bred out again. All we may be observing is that the particular gene, which causes broad-headedness, does not flourish in this country. Ridgeway, long ago drew attention to this phenomenon and stated categorically that skull shapes could change very much in a single generation. Or, in other words, that skull measurements were not the slightest value for determining the origin of a people. While this probably goes a little too far, it is a theory which cannot be easily neglected. The Beaker people may still have formed an important part of the stock of the Iron Age, Romano-British or Anglo-Saxon people; although the predominant skull form had become that known as 'coffin-shaped'. Only by the other contents of a grave is it possible to tell whether its occupant was a Romano-British or an Anglo-Saxon. Inferences drawn from the measurement of skulls should not be accepted as facts without considerable hesitation.

It is impossible to say therefore whether the Beaker people survived in the population and married into that of the Celtic Iron Age immigrants or not. If they did not, then these Celtic immigrants reintroduced the worship of Gog and Magog. It seems more probable, however, that they found it already here amongst the former Bronze Age inhabitants. They also believed in the same religion themselves. The worship of the sun was evidently of great importance in Bronze Age Britain, for nothing but the strongest religious feelings could have caused the transportation of the 'Blue' stones at Stonehenge, the spotted diorite circle, from the Prescelly mountain in Pembrokeshire, to the middle of Salisbury Plain. That these same ideas persisted without a break into the Celtic Iron Age is more or less proved by the Iron Age pottery found in the empty holes of the two outer rings at Stonehenge. Much Iron Age pottery has also been found in Scottish circles on top of the original fragments left there by the Beaker people who set up the stones. It looks very much, therefore, as if we may assume that there was no break in the tradition of religious observance. The Maypole dance may well carry on a customary ritual, which has scarcely changed since 1800 B.C. This is why it is important to see what lies beneath, or outside, the traditional sites of Maypole dances.

Still, all this has brought us little nearer to the answer of where this kind of religion originated. The late Sir James Frazer, in his *Golden Bough*, investigated the dates of Celtic Festivals. May 1st and November 1st were the two most important. These, in his opinion, could only have been chosen by a pastoral people, as opposed to an agricultural one. This is clearly correct, but we must go further than this. The dates could only have been chosen by a people who lived in a hilly or mountainous district. On May 1st they moved their grazings up into the mountain pastures. On November 1st they killed off all the animals for which they could not provide food for the winter. The custom of driving the cattle up in summer to the shieling, airidh, havod or settr was universal in the hill countries of north-western Europe. It may well have been evolved in the Alpine region and carried from there by the earliest metal-using races to arrive in the north-west.

Perhaps then we should look for the answer of our problem somewhere to the east of the Alps, north of the Adriatic and south of the great forests, where Diana obtained her reindeer. On the great trade route from south to north, which Mr. J. M. de Navarro identified in his *Amber Routes*, merchants began to move in the earliest Bronze Age. Along this road Hercules may have passed on his visit to the distant Cimmerians; up it Ulysses strode in search of the people who could not distinguish an oar from a winnowing-fan. The merchants, enjoying the peace which was granted in Antiquity to all genuine travellers, talked of their gods to the pastoral peoples of the Alpine foot-hills and in particular of the worship of the sun and his continual war against his enemy the night. Herdsmen are not confined to daylight in their activities, as are pure agriculturalists. They added the moon to the story, for her light was as important to them as the light of the sun. And so the belief and story grew, to spread to lands far beyond the wildest dreams of the people who created it. Till men who looked out in winter over the Baltic Ice, or the distant Cairn Gorms, believed the same doc-trine and performed the same ceremony as those who lived beneath the high sun of India, or by the olive groves of Greece.

There is one great obstacle to this idea, which is, I think, fatal. The men who worshipped the sun and moon in Scandinavia were obviously boatmen. They used boats of a type by no means unlike those used on the coasts of Syria and Palestine at more or less the same time. They must have reached their northern homes going most of the way by water. They cannot have been an inland people. Some authorities look for the home of the Aryans in the lands north of the Black Sea; others seek them in Persia and Asia Minor. Although the Caucasus foothills would answer many of our requirements, I feel that there is nothing to show that peoples living there evolved this type of ship, or even used ships at all. Russians have never been celebrated for their seamanship. I shall therefore take a brief look at Asia Minor.

In our investigation into the origins of Gog and Magog, it is necessary to pay particular attention to the remarks made about them by Ezekiel (*supra*, p. 10, Ezekiel xxiii). Since nobody today can possibly hope to have expert knowledge over anything but a relatively small field, I have been compelled to make great use of the authorities in the *Cambridge Ancient History* and the eleventh edition of the *Encyclopaedia Britannica*. The articles on subjects about which I know a little are so good in this edition that I feel the same must be the case in others.

Ezekiel was clearly expecting an invasion of Palestine led by the people of Gog. Ezekiel was a Hebrew priest, who was among those carried into captivity by Nebuchadnezzar about 600 B.C., and gave out his prophecy shortly after this. In point of fact, it seems that the invasion never took place. Although Libya and

Ethiopia are mentioned among the enemies, it is clear that the expected attack was to be from the north. Gog is the chief prince of Tubal and Meshech. Tubal is in the hills to the north of Syria. Persia, to the north-east, is coming and so is Gomer on the head-waters of the Euphrates. These were peoples of the old Hatti group of the Hittite empire and their language was Aryan, or Indo-European. These were a people who had worshipped Baal from a very early time. Baal was apparently a god of the powers of nature and Astarte, or Ashtoreth was his wife. The indecencies connected with their worship made as great an impression on the Old Testament prophets as the holocausts, connected with the later worship at Carthage, made on Classical writers. In both cases there is some propaganda in the writings. Baal worship was widespread among the Hebrews, while the Carthaginians had been great rivals of Rome and of Greece before her.

There seems to be no real objection to the view that Baal was a sun god and Astarte a moon goddess. There were many little local varieties of Baal, who appear in the Bible in the plural as baalim. These were probably offshoots from the original belief due to the collapse of the Hittite Empire, which was apparently at the height of its power about 1300 B.C. There seems to have been no similar break-up of the worship of Astarte. She remained the great Earth Mother goddess and became Diana of the Ephesians. It is thought by some that the name Baal was derived from the Celtic Bel, meaning the 'shining one'. This incidentally is the epithet applied to Siva.

Now in Syria, in the Jebel-el-Druz area, lived Og, the king of Bashan. He was a giant and his city or land was Ashtaroth. It may be just a coincidence that he was a giant and that his name was Og: but, when he is also found associated with Ashtaroth, the great Mother Goddess who, in later times at any rate, was also a moon goddess, there are too many coincidences. Og must be the same as Gog, Ashtaroth the same as Magog and Baal, Og.

If Baal really was named from a Celtic Bel, then many things fall into place with a click. Belenus was the Gaulish Sun God. Beltane was the great May Day festival, on which bale fires were lighted. Balor, the Irish god on Tory Island, who, when his eye was opened with a hook, burnt people up, as Siva did. There are many of these phenomena and all are well known. But there is more to it than that, for when Solomon's friend, Hiram King of Tyre, built his great temple to Baal, the god was apparently depicted in the guise of Hercules. The Gaulish Hercules, moreover, was known as Ogmius and the Irish one as Ogma Sunface. Remembering that Harold Bayley has no hesitation in referring Og and Gog, ogle, goggle and giggle to the same root, I have none in equating Ogmius with Gog and thus with Baal.

So it seems that Helith, the Cerne Giant, is both Helith and Gog. He is both Hercules and Baal. He represents the sun. His name, Helith, is both a Gaulish form of Hercules and a Celtic variant of the Greek Helios, the sun. It is no wonder then that at Beltane, the great May Day festival, a Maypole should have been set up in honour of the sun and also to promote fertility.

However, there is no certainty in thinking that the worship of Baal originated in Asia Minor, for the Hatti are thought by many, like the Indo-Europeans in India or Britain, to have come from somewhere else. Where they came from can only be guessed; but I am ready to believe that it was no great distance away. Sun and Moon religions tended to originate in this part of the world.

Chapter Seven

THIS seems to be a good point at which to try to summarize what available information there is bearing on the character of this ancient religion. Fortunately so much has been collected, particularly by Sir James Frazer in the *Golden Bough*, that it is not necessary to tramp about the country asking questions. The information is there for those who care to seek it.

The interpretation of this collected information is always a matter of personal opinion. Having seen the great success obtained by Colonel Alfred Burne, by his use of what he terms 'Inherent Military Probability' in the study of ancient warfare, I now make considerable use of 'Inherent Probability' in other matters. It is really only a question of using common sense to think out what ordinary people would normally do under given conditions. Although, therefore, I am about to set out what I think was the underlying Aryan belief and ritual, this is no more than what I think it must have been after considering the evidence. It is a verdict based on circumstantial evidence alone. No one can prove whether it is true or not; because nobody will ever be able to do more than make an estimate.

The worship of Gog and Magog was invented by a pastoral people, whose whole livelihood was bound up with the welfare of their flocks and herds; but it evolved in a purely pastoral existence and became modified by the introduction of agriculture. To begin with, the fertility of the flocks and herds were all-important. The beasts all had mothers. There must be a great mother for everything. This was Mother Earth, the great mother of all nature. But every mother animal needed the services of a male before she could become fertile. There had to be a Great Father also. In these early times the mother was more important than the father. This was probably due to the

111

widespread primitive lack of understanding of the processes of parenthood. Nobody quite knew who the father was. For this reason a woman was the head of the tribe; although she might rule through her consort. The royal line of the Picts in Scotland descended through the queens and their daughters down to the seventh century of our era and was noted by Bede. Therefore the chief power of nature was a Mother Goddess. Among the Indo-Europeans the word 'Ma' meant 'Mother' and still does. Baal, among the early Hittites at about 1300 B.C., was apparently a female goddess of fertility: only at some later stage did Baal become male. The Earth Mother was not at first associated with the moon, but was regarded as a great cow, or great sheep. But the summer sun was recognized as the source of necessary heat and light, which made the grass grow on which animals lived. He then made the Earth Mother fertile. He was the father. It was only reasonable to think so. Well then, if the sun was the Great Father, what was that other great, round, shining thing, which appeared at regular intervals and enabled you to estimate the passage of the seasons? Of course that must be the Great Mother. She did not live in the Earth after all, but up in the sky where she could see all that was going on. Was not her sign on the head of every sheep and cow? The Moon was of course the Mother. 'Why had we not thought of it before?'

But, although the sun and moon were regular in their appearances and almost always turned up when they were expected, every now and then a terrible black hand seemed to stretch out and take hold of them. This dreadful black thing made the world feel cold when he did this to the sun. Everything felt uncanny when this happened on a bright summer's day. The sun had always got away so far and so had the moon, but it might not always happen thus. This terrible dark power must be an enemy of the great, good, shining ones. He must be the father of wolves, lions and other evil things, which preyed on the flocks and herds. Just as man was always at war with the wolves to protect his stock, so were the sun and moon always at war with this black thing, which seemed to be round too. It was trying to stop all light, all life and all reproduction. Something must be done to help the sun and moon. The thing could only be done by sympathetic magic. People must dance in a ring to keep the sun and moon spinning on their courses and copy the process of procreation to aid them in that respect. The Black Demon had to be destroyed by the sun and moon. The only way that this could be aided was to destroy something evil in their own community. From this it all grew.

In southern lands, where agriculture was largely practised and stock-rearing was of less account, the moon tended to drop out of the picture and the sun became much more important. The farmer was not out at night scaring wolves away and looking after calving cows. He did not need the light of the moon. The sun took over most of the business of ensuring the food supply. He made the crops grow by his warmth. Baal became a sun god amongst the Phoenicians. The Assyrian sun god, Ashur, was the hero in the war against Tiamat the power of darkness. Siva is more powerful than his wife, Maha-devi.

The myth of the sun and moon's struggle against the demon of darkness went with the Aryans on all their migrations and spread from them to other races, who added some of their own ideas to the main story. It reached Britain at least fifteen hundred years before the Birth of Christ and traces of its ritual performance still remain with us.

In the early Bronze Age, Britain appears to have had a more or less universal religious organization, which resulted in the same kind of religious buildings everywhere. The organization was so powerful that it could order the removal of a particularly sacred stone circle from Pembrokeshire and its transport to Stonehenge. The circular stone temples seem clearly connected with the worship of the sun and the numerous cup markings found on many of the Scottish circles link them with the cult of the moon. Since, as we have already seen, the cult was also practised by the Celts, it seems evident that there was no break in its ritual performance. The priestly caste of the Celts were the Druids, and so it seems probable that the Druidic priesthood evolved from simple beginnings during the Bronze and Iron Ages, until it became the most powerful force of its kind in the west. It is legitimate then to add what we know about the Druids to the information, which can be obtained from other sources, about the rites connected with the worship of sun and moon. Caesar believed that Druidism originated in Britain.

First then, the main belief centred round the certainty of a reincarnation, or rather transmigration, of the soul. Death was not the end of life; it was just the gate to another. It did not matter killing people: you might be hurting them, but they were not destroyed. Since we have seen reason for thinking that the Aryan religion had one common source and was fundamentally the same from India to Britain; since the Druids and the Brahmins both had to learn an enormous mass of verses relating to their faith and philosophy by heart, and since the Brahmin verses were written down in Sanskrit some six hundred years before the Birth of Christ, it seems reasonable to suppose that these verses might be closely similar in the two areas. In the *Bhagavad-Gita*, as translated by Swami Prabhavananda and Chrisopher Isherwood, the general idea of this doctrine is given as follows:

'Just as the dweller in this body passes through childhood, youth and old age, so at death he merely passes into another kind of body . . .

'Bodies are said to die, but that which possesses the body is eternal. It cannot be limited, or destroyed. Therefore you must fight . . .

'Happy are the warriors to whom a battle such as this comes: it opens a door to heaven . . .

'Die, and you win heaven. Conquer, and you enjoy the earth. Stand up now, Son of Kunti, and resolve to fight. Realize that pleasure and pain, gain and loss, victory and defeat, are all one and the same: then go into battle.'

If this was the kind of creed taught by the Druids, and it seems most probable that this was the case, it is no wonder that the Romans hastily suppressed it. Few doctrines could have been more dangerous in the event of a revolt against Rome. It explains too the speed and fury of Boadicea's revolt and why she did not hesitate to sacrifice her captives to Adraste.[1] But this creed explains the curious lack of staying power in the wars between the Celts and Romans. This was no doctrine of 'stand

[1] Adraste is a puzzling name. Adrastia was a nurse to Jupiter and the Egyptians told that she was placed above the moon to watch the affairs of men. It seems probable that there was some confusion over this name and that it was either Astarte, or a Celtic version of Baal's wife.

fast and stick it out'. It encouraged a furious charge; but, if this failed, it did not seem worth going on with it, for 'victory and defeat, are all one and the same'. This philosophy lost Gaul and most of Britain to the Roman invaders.

The Druids were great students of the heavenly bodies. Their main deduction from this appears to have been that the sun and moon were the great arbiters of the affairs of men and that they were continually at war with the power of Darkness. To further the successes of their two great gods in this struggle, they maintained the two pastoral festivals of Beltane and Hallowe'en. In other parts of Europe the great festival days became changed to Midsummer and Midwinter, which fitted more into the ways of the husbandman. In Britain, France, Scandinavia and some other areas, the festivals remained as they had always been. Some of the dates are now a little out, probably owing to the reform of the Calendar. For instance Helith's festival, the Flory or Furry, at Helston in Cornwall, is now held on May 8th. Generally speaking Beltane was fixed to the beginning of May and Hallowe'en to the beginning of November.

Both ceremonies included a bonfire, a ring dance, general licence and a feast. They might also be accompanied by public games, such as horse racing, or wrestling. At some of them a ritual was performed in which the sun god overcame the demon of darkness; or the moon goddess progressed across the Heavens.

In the country districts, where pastoral pursuits were important, the cattle were either passed through the smoke of the bonfire or made to look at it. Frazer's investigations made it quite clear that the choice of a sacrificial human victim, who was subsequently burnt in the bonfire, was implied by the old Beltane customs in Scotland. He was inclined to believe that all this bonfire ceremony was intended to purify the cattle and the people themselves from the spells of witches. Witches could make both human beings and their animals barren. The fire freed them from this curse. I think the rite had rather a different origin. It seems more probable that it should be taken as part of the whole ritual on that festival and as sympathetic magic to aid the sun and moon in their war against the powers of Darkness. The ring dance was to aid the heavenly bodies in their passage through the sky. The circular trench, with the bonfire in the middle, on which the sacrifice was burnt,[1] represented the sun destroying the victim, who was chosen to represent the demon of darkness. It helped the sun to destroy the real demon. The smell of the fire and its burning victim passed on to and would cling to the people and cattle and so be a warning to the emissaries of the evil powers, whether they were witches or wolves, to keep away. Thus it answered the purpose of purification and all would be fertile. The excitement, rejoicing and burning of the Guy on November the fifth shows how deeply the whole thing was implanted in popular memory. Brutal though the whole ritual seems to us, it must be borne in mind that everybody concerned firmly believed that they were only passing the victim through the door into another existence. The more it hurt the poor wretch, the more it would hurt the demon of Darkness. It is evident that where possible the sacrifice would either be a suspected witch or a malefactor. The fact that the person chosen, by lot in some of the Highland Beltane ceremonies, was known as a 'cailleach', which means an 'old woman', whether he was a man or woman, shows that this was the case. If you could not burn the demon himself, you could at least burn one of his followers. It was just unfortunate if there were no real witches available. Someone had to do instead and you chose him fairly by drawing lots.

When their astrological studies, or perhaps some more obvious facts, told the Druids that real trouble was in the offing, they staged a really big dose of sympathetic magic to help the sun and moon. They built a huge wicker representation of the demon, filled it with felons, or prisoners of war, and burnt the whole thing. This was only the Beltane or Hallowe'en sacrifice on a large scale. No doubt it made an unpleasant impression on the Romans, not because they minded cruelty, but because it was just the kind of thing that their Carthaginian enemies, worshippers of Baal, had done also. They passed children through the fire to Moloch. The Romans had given up human sacrifices themselves, but knew well enough that they had once practised them.

[1] It seems at least curious that the word 'Hell', which was used to describe the place of torment for the wicked, should supposedly be derived from the old English 'hel' to cover. The symptoms of those in torment appear to resemble closely those of the victims offered to Helith. 'If you do not respect the laws of Holy Church, you will go to Helith and be burnt in everlasting torment.'

But it was not because they went in for human sacrifice that the druid caste were so rigorously crushed. Other gods in Gaul were worshipped with human sacrifices and still survived far into Roman times. The trouble with the Druids was that they trained the warlike youths of the chieftain class to a doctrine, which encouraged them to reckless courage in war. It was a form of teaching which could not be allowed in lands not completely pacified and assimilated.

Lastly, the feast and general licence was also magic. It was designed to assist the sun and moon in securing fertility to all, by representing the sacred marriage of sun and moon.

Thus the religious ceremony, although it was a combination of several religious features, had only one aim. This was the general productivity of the earth, man and beast. It was to be obtained by assisting the sun and moon in the performance of their work and in preventing the powers of darkness from interfering with it.

Somewhere into this picture fits the idea of cremating the dead. It was a universal practice in Britain, for the whole of the Bronze Age and much of the Iron Age, to burn the dead on a pyre, which looks from its surroundings much the same as the Beltane bonfire. It was enclosed in a circular trench and often in a ring of wooden posts. I have not done much barrow digging myself and have only excavated or helped to direct the excavation of some sixteen barrows or cairns. All of these, except three, were surrounded by a circular trench and two had an inner ring of post holes. One barrow contained the cremated remains of a priest or witch doctor, for beside the urn, which contained his ashes, had been placed a small bag containing two bone tubes, which are precisely similar to tubes used by African witch doctors for disguising their voices when speaking for the gods.[1] These tubes, covered at one end with a membrane, were pushed up the witch doctor's nostril with remarkable results. This particular magician was also provided with a set of ten pointed bones, all of which, except one, had a small hole at the blunt end. These were presumably used for drawing lots. A second witch doctor's cremation was probably found by Sir Cyril Fox in a barrow at Barton Mills. There he found a set of four rectangular bone slabs, each perforated transversely with

[1] *Cambridge Antiquarian Society Proceedings*, vol. xliii, p. 48, Fig. 11 (Nos. 3 and 4).

three holes for stringing.[1] These again are strikingly similar to sets of four rectangular bones used by African witch doctors.

It seems evident then that there is some connection between the Beltane fire ritual and the rite of cremation. Both took place within a ditch, which presumably represented a sun symbol. Each fire was at one time used to burn somebody. Sometimes the burnt man was a priest or witch doctor. The rite of cremation may, in fact, be an offshoot from the solar ritual sacrifice. Associated with the idea that burning a victim led to the general fertility of everything, the ashes of the corpse were covered with a round mound to represent the breast of Mother Earth. It is quite possible that some of our Bronze Age barrows are the actual graves of the sacrificial victims of the Beltane or Hallowe'en festivals.

The one ritual performed by the Druids, which has actually come down to us in full description from Classical antiquity, was the cutting of the mistletoe when it was found growing on an oak tree. Much heavy weather has been encountered by people making attempts to explain this apparently childish performance. I think, however, that it is capable of a simple explanation. Once again this is only opinion, but it appears to make complete sense. The pearl was always a symbol of the moon in the Celtic west; the moon being the Pearl of Heaven. The mistletoe was a living pearl. The oak was the tree of the Celtic Jupiter, who was the sun god (Celtic statuettes have been found showing him both with the solar wheel symbol and a thunderbolt). When, therefore, the moon's living pearl was found as a rarity growing on the sun's sacred tree, it was clear evidence that the sacred marriage of sun and moon had actually taken place. What could be a more happy augury for the future fertility of man and beast. The moon's sacred white oxen, with her symbol denoted by their horns, were at once brought and sacrificed. The mistletoe was cut with a golden lunar sickle and collected with the greatest care to prevent it being soiled in any way.

The name Druid is in any case connected with the Gaulish 'Dru', an oak. It is remarkable, as I learnt from Donald A. Mackenzie, in his *Ancient Man in Britain*, that Galatian (Gaulish) religious centre in Asia Minor was called Drunemeton,

---

[1] *Cambridge Antiquarian Society Proceedings*, vol. xxvi, p. 34, Fig. 4.

which may be translated as the sacred oak grove. But the
nemeton part of this name is certainly connected with the
moon. Nem or nemh is heaven or heavenly. In Gaelic a pearl is
sometimes called neamhnuid. The moon is the pearl of heaven;
so there is a clear relationship between nemeton and the moon.
A west-country goddess in Roman Britain was Nemetona, who
must have been a moon goddess and a goddess of the sacred
woodland, an Artemis or Diana. From this, owing to the
extreme sagacity of Sir Cyril and Lady Fox, I think we can
locate one of the great sites of sun and moon worship in Britain.
The story is worth telling, because it shows what can be done
by archaeological reasoning without ever touching a spade at
all. I must say that any blame attaching to the identification of
their discovery as a former Druidic religious site is mine: Sir
Cyril Fox, as long as I can remember and that must be some
thirty-two years, has always laid great stress on the importance
of a detailed study of maps. In particular he hammered into my
thick head the value of examining parish boundaries; these being
normally at least a thousand years old. A long straight stretch
appearing on the maps of several adjacent parishes was almost
certain to mark the course of an ancient road. This, as it happens,
is not infallible, but it is a very good guide. Poring over the
six-inch maps of mid-Devon, Sir Cyril and Lady Fox picked up
a straight line of parish boundaries running approximately east
to west, till they hit and crossed the river Taw some five miles
north-east of Okehampton. Going out from Exeter, they walked
along the line of parish boundaries and soon realized that they
had stumbled on the course of an unknown Roman road. There
was no doubt about it; it was, as I have seen, a well-constructed,
metalled road running through rather damp pasture land. When
the road neared the Taw they made a second discovery. Close
beside the road and adjacent to the ford or bridge, which must
have crossed the river, was a large unknown Roman fortress,
with bastions at its corners. There, in spite of air photography
and all other present-day aids, was a completely unguessed
military road and fortress. What was it?

An ancient document, known as the Ravenna Cosmography,
gives some lists of places in Britain west of Exeter. Few of these
have even been guessed. But, after poring over the maps, one
at once caught the eye of the Foxes. This was Nemeto Statio.

The reason why it caught their eye was that all round their new road and fort were villages which seemed to bear this name in a slightly decayed form. There were Nymets and Nymphs in considerable numbers. Whatever others may think, Inherent Probability has no doubt about putting the name of Nemeto Statio on the newly found fort.

This was all woodland in the old days and the Nymets and Nymphs must have been clearings in a sacred forest. Somewhere, probably near Nemeto Statio, the moon's living pearl had been found on the sun's sacred oak.

However, it was all apparently a Gog and Magog country. Hell Tor and Mardon (Ma-don) with their giants are not far away. Okehampton, with its giglet fair, both names equated with Gog by Harold Bayley, is only five miles distant. Belstone Tor, Baal or Belenus' stone, overlooks it. While hanging on the sides of the gorge of the river Teign are the great Iron Age fortresses of Prestonbury and Cranbrook. Whether Drewsteignton has anything to do with the Druids, I leave readers to guess for themselves.

Traces of this old religion are still visible everywhere in Britain. Most superstitions are relics of old religious ritual and I will discuss some of them in a moment. There are, however, active survivals from the rituals themselves.

The ritual connected with the sacred marriage of the sun and moon has been transferred from Beltane to the agriculturalist's mid-winter ceremony of Christmas. Christmas is known to have been deliberately transferred from the pagan mid-winter festivities of Sol Invictus, the unconquerable sun. At Christmas, any man may kiss any woman under the moon's sacred mistletoe. This licence is a pale echo of the orgies of Artemis.

I do not know whether Beltane fires are lit anywhere to-day. The ceremony is mostly preserved in a very attentuated form at Coronations, which are usually welcomed with a feast and bonfire. Hallowe'en has been more fortunate in having been given a splendid substitute for the demon of darkness in the shape of Guy Fawkes. All attempts to reduce this ceremony to complete respectability fail.

Ring dances still survive, particularly in Scotland, and are greeted with appropriate shouting and rejoicing. They are chiefly associated with the mid-winter season.

Hogmanay, the last night of the year, preserved in the Highlands of Scotland a ceremony which must have belonged once to Hallowe'en, the Celtic New Year's Eve. I do not expect that this custom can still be found. A man, dressed in a bull's hide, had to run sunways round the house and then pronounce a blessing on the inmates and their cattle. He then burnt some hairs from the bull's hide in the fire and all the people in the house, together with their domestic animals, had to smell it. The whole performance was accompanied by racing and chasing, shouting and din. Till relatively recent times, the cattle byre was a part of the house so that the beasts could see the fire. This ceremony is clearly much the same, and for the same purpose, as that performed at Beltane. The man was aiding the sun by his circular run and ran under the cow's horns symbol of the moon. The smell of the sacrificial victim had to pass on man and beast to ensure their fertility.

Maypoles are occasionally set up on Beltane, but only as a pretty custom. Such festivities as the Helston Flory have been revived. Some processions, however, seem to be quite spontaneous and the choice of Labour Day as the first of May must surely be due to a general feeling that the day ought to be celebrated. So we see that none of the pagan rites is quite dead.

When we come to the realms of superstition the list is very great and I shall only mention those that I happen to know for myself and not look up any at all. Most of them relate to the moon.

First of all, the moon is still vaguely believed to be capable of conferring benefits on those who offer her homage. You can ask a wish the first time you see any new moon, but you must bow to her. The first moon of the year is the most lucky. Of course this should be the first moon in November, but now it is the first in January. It is believed to be unlucky to see the moon through glass or through a tree. Although the glass probably referred to a looking-glass, in which the crescent moon appeared unfortunately to be waning; it is clear that it was unlucky that anything should hide even part of the moon's face from you when you bowed to her. If she hid her face, it was a sign of her displeasure. You find mention of this sign of displeasure on the part of the Deity in the Bible. Homage therefore was widely paid to the moon on its first appearance in every month and particularly at about Hallowe'en.

The moon's light falling on a sleeping person is still believed to make them mad. The reason for this is not hard to seek. If a person were asleep when the moon rose and shone on him, he could not bow to her in respect and therefore was guilty of great disrespect. In the days of windowless houses this cannot have happened very often. No doubt people, sleeping in the open, were careful in their choice of site. If one of these was so lazy and irreverent as not to do so, he must have been mad.

The moon's symbol, in the form of a horseshoe, was considered necessary above the door of house and byre. Plenty are still nailed up for luck. Some maintain that they should be hung horns downwards over a peg as symbols of fertility. The majority, however, believe that the moon's horns should be upward.

It is still lucky to pick up the moon's symbol in a field. This entitles the finder to a wish from the moon; but whether it will be granted or not can only be judged by augury. The horseshoe is thrown backwards over the finder's left shoulder and whether the horns point towards or away from him shows whether the wish will be granted. I cannot remember, but I think the horns should point towards you.

The moon's horseshoe symbol still plays an important part in our marriage customs. It can frequently be observed on the back of the bridal car, which takes the newly married couple away on their honeymoon. Since both sun and moon were necessary for a fruitful marriage, the sun is still remembered in the saying, 'Happy is the bride on whom the sun shines.'

Much of the everyday life of Britain is still riddled with superstitions relating to the moon, for as the great Earth Mother she was more important than the sun. The white horse was one of her symbols and you must call it grey so as not to speak of her directly. If you see a grey horse, you can ask the moon for a wish, but you must do so before you think of the horse's tail. Not only would it be disrespectful to think of that end of the horse, it would also be useless if the goddess were turning her face from you.

The moon's protective symbol, in the form of a horse's head or a horseshoe, still appears on many of the brass pendants, which are worn by our cart and draught horses. Many are just a sickle moon itself. Some importance may have been attached to the fact that when a simple representation of the moon is displayed, the horns are upward; when the symbol is a horse-shoe the horns are placed downwards. The one may attempt to attract the general bounty expected from the new moon; while the other may draw more attention to the fertility side of the matter. An occasional brass may exhibit a fish on its disc. This is probably not a Christian symbol, but that of the moon goddess, Astarte. Stories of ghosts of white horses still appear to cling to places where worship must have once taken place.

The moon goddess played a great part in the superstitions of fishermen and in that of sailors generally. She was believed to be able to bring back lost ships; for, ever since the days of the Bronze Age men in Scandinavia, ships have been associated with her. Ghosts of missing vessels revisit the glimpses of the moon. I have described a number of these sea superstitions in *Boats and Boatmen*, and there is no need to repeat them here. I shall, however, mention the 'oculus'. This is the eye, which is still found painted on either bow of ships all over Europe and Asia. In ancient Egypt this eye apparently ensured the presence and protection of the sun; but this appears to have changed to the eye of Isis and thus of the moon. With the coming of Christianity, many of these eyes were changed to the 'Stella Maris' of the Virgin Mary. Some, however, would maintain that the word Mary is really related to the Ma of the Great Mother and thus Magog. The oculus has still not entirely deserted our fishing fleets. This year, 1955, I noticed a Stella Maris on the bow of a West Highland boat; the square and compasses, a masonic sign, but here a degenerate oculus, on the bow of a Balantrae vessel; and several scrolls of oculus form on Banffshire seine fishermen. Not long ago I saw a degenerate oculus on the bow of a Lewis boat, which was composed of the moon's swan and Astarte's fish.

The Blessing of the French fishing fleets is, as I have shown elsewhere,[1] taken directly from the ritual performed in honour of Isis at the opening of the ancient sailing season. It is not far-fetched to see the same idea beneath the yearly civic opening of the oyster fishery. In fact, we may say that the powers of the moon are still requested to secure the harvest of the sea.

[1] T. C. Lethbridge, *Boats and Boatmen*.

When we turn to the affairs of the agriculturalist, the story is the same. All over the land one finds the belief that seeds planted with a waning moon will not prosper. The moon is going away and, like the passing grey horse, cannot be expected to give aid to the growing crop. To this is sometimes added that root crops should be planted with a waning moon. The explanation for this appears to be that originally it was believed that the moon disappeared into the earth. Therefore, if you wanted crops to grow high, you planted them when the moon was about to grow to her full strength in the sky; but if you wished them to grow downwards, you sent them to follow her into the earth.

Finally, the peat in the Highlands must be cut when the moon is right. If not, it will never dry properly and will smoke.

In fact, there are many more customs with us today in relation to the moon than to anything else. This could only be the case if she had once been the most important religious factor in the whole of Britain for a very long period of time. The cults of the gods of the Norseman have gone almost without trace. They were not particularly intelligent conceptions in any case, whereas there was much sound reasoning at the back of this cult of fertility and transmigration. More than anything else the survival of such widespread traces of the worship of sun and moon, Gog and Magog, or whatever names you like to choose for them, demonstrates the impossibility of the idea that the Romano-British population was exterminated by the Anglo-Saxons. It was not even driven out of London. For at least three thousand five hundred years this religion was practised in this country and before we leave it we must try to estimate whether it still exists in the land as a living doctrine.

To do this we must look at a secret religion, which is known to be still practised. I refer, of course, to the cult, which is generally termed that of the witches. Dr. Margaret Murray is the great worker on this subject and no one can attempt to form an opinion on the matter, without making a close study of her books, *The God of the Witches* and *The Witch Cult in Western Europe*. In these she has rightly concentrated on the essential features of the religion and not earned easy money by dwelling too much on the malignant and often absurd side of it, when it got into the hands of moral degenerates. Dr. Murray traces the cult far back into the Stone Age, perhaps more than ten thousand years ago, when men were hunters and nothing else. It is clear, however, that it only came into full being when a pastoral stage of existence had largely replaced the hunting as a mode of life. Its main function was to promote the fertility of man and beast. In order to secure this end, ritual dances were performed, ritual licence and feast took place and at intervals victims were put to death by fire. It is known that the chief object of adoration is a goddess, but I have never seen her name disclosed, although something resembling 'Adraste' has been suggested. The leader of the ceremonies, however, seems frequently to have been dressed up to resemble a bull, goat or horse and I get the impression that he was under the guise of one of the moon's symbolic animals. Now this ritual bears a close resemblance to that deduced for our Gog and Magog religion. Is it the same or not?

The chief difficulty is that the fire ceremonies of Beltane, Hallowe'en and the rest, were almost universally described as being intended to prevent witchcraft and as charms against witches. If that is so, then the witch cult was hostile to that of Gog and Magog. This interpretation, however, may not necessarily be correct, or it may only indicate some heretical or schismatic rift. The term witch may have been wrongly interpreted and be better explained as demon, jinn or some similar supernatural child of darkness. The information concerning the witch cult collected by Dr. Murray, is almost entirely drawn from the records of its enemies in the Christian church, who were trying to stamp it out. Thus the priest of each coven is always known as a devil.

The chief areas in which the witch cult flourished in Britain were East Anglia, the West Country, the counties around Lancashire and the east of Scotland. In East Anglia lived the great tribe of the Iceni, who I believe to have been 'horse' people. On the edge of their territory we find this Gog and Magog myth story. On the coins of their Catuvellaunian neighbours are numerous pictures of horses and moons. Superstitions relating to the moon are still very prevalent. In the West Country we have a mass of giant stories; places named after Helith; survivals of May Day festivals; numerous superstitions related to the moon both on land and sea. In the Lancashire area horse superstitions are numerous. In the eastern Scottish area we find the greatest collection of cup markings in the stone circles and, later by more than a thousand years, an enormous number of moon symbols carved on the so-called 'Pictish' stones. The Pictish crown also descended in the female line. Here the oculus survives strongly on the bows of boats.

While noting that the witch cult was found outside these areas, at the same time it is remarkable that it appears to coincide with other indications of ancient moon worship. In the west Highlands there is less evidence for organized pagan religion at any time. There were apparently no covens and few 'Pictish' stones.

The witch cult was deeply rooted in popular belief. So was the Gog and Magog religion. What we know of the witch cult reveals the same rite of dancing in a ring to aid the heavenly bodies in their journeys; the same belief in the method to be employed in increasing fertility of man and beast; the same ritual feasting; the same method of sacrifice by fire and the apparent employment of lunar symbolism by the officiating priest. On the opposite side we can only place the widespread belief that the Beltane fires were made against the witches.

There is little to suggest that, in the witch ritual, the sun was regarded as being as important as the moon. The same is true of popular superstitions today. Very few seem to relate to the sun. Only two occur to me at the moment. One is that it is unlucky to be overshadowed by somebody, or to step on his shadow. This, of course, is similar to the obscuring of the moon. The sun's face was hidden from you. In the second superstition you can obtain a wish by looking at the sun through the hole in a pebble, which you have found by chance. It is the lucky solar equivalent of the lunar horseshoe. The god or goddess has permitted you to find the symbol to indicate their presence.

On the whole then, until somebody can advance substantial proof that it is not the case, Inherent Probability tells us that the witch cult and the worship of Gog and Magog are one and the same. The interpretation of the Beltane fires as being made against witches has somehow become distorted. This may well be the case for, as the witch cult was slowly crushed, its devotees turned more and more to the practice of black magic against its enemies. Much of the Druidic lore in this respect would probably have been available to them. The witch cult no doubt degenerated under ceaseless persecution; but I think we should find that, if we could see a true account of their beliefs, we should discover that they contained many things still to be found in the teaching of the Brahmins in India.

The popular picture of witches, which still remains with us to-day, is the result of long and furious propaganda by their enemies. It must be far from the truth. A faith, which needed so much venom from ecclesiastical authority to suppress it, must have had many good points in order to make it a serious rival. It is clear, for instance, that it had a firm belief in immortality and this probably carried with it the idea of the transmigration of souls. I should imagine that the animal familiars, which the witches cherished, were undoubtedly regarded as human beings in another bodily form.

The witches believed so firmly in their religion that they were quite ready to die for it and apparently happy to do so as long as they were burnt. By being burnt they became the sacrificial victim, aiding their deity in the struggle against the powers of darkness and ensuring fertility to their neighbours.

These victims were seldom the toothless hags, mumbling in the corner of a hovel over a toad, that we have been brought up to imagine. They were frequently young and cheerful girls. Although I know little about them that I have not learnt from Dr. Murray, either by word of mouth or from her books, I can see that there was something here that we might well respect. The devotees of this cult showed a steadiness, literally under fire, which, however misguided their ideas may have been, had a nobility of its own. It is perhaps no coincidence that one of the commonest 'witch' names was Margaret and means a 'Pearl'.

Chapter Eight

OUR investigation appears to have led us back to an earlier and perhaps purer stage of a religious belief, than that studied by Sir James Frazer in *The Golden Bough*. His dying god, the burning of the nature spirit and all the rest of it, may well be the result of an adaptation of the earlier beliefs of a pastoral people in an agricultural age. In Britain there seems to have been less of this than elsewhere. This may be the reason why Caesar, who was evidently most interested in the subject, said that Druidism was found in its purest form in Britain.

The religion, perhaps in a very primitive form, reached Britain at least fifteen hundred years before the Birth of Christ. Before Agamemnon hauled up his curved ships and invested Troy; before Ulysses sailed to Ogygia, which some believe to have been Ireland, men in Britain were worshipping Gog and Magog; the words presumably meaning no more than God and Mother God. Whether these people spoke a primitive form of the Celtic language, nobody knows. That they were a very early Celtic wave seems most probable. That they were herdsmen, of the type by whom the religion was evolved, is certain. There is no reason to suppose that any other radically different belief was introduced during the full Bronze Age which followed. We shall not, however, really be in a position to judge this until some attempt is made to find and excavate the most important Bronze Age city in all western Europe. Till Tartessus, the Tarshish of the Bible, is explored, no one can possibly judge what religions came into Britain by the Atlantic sea route. Tartessus was somewhere at the junction of two rivers on the south-west coast of Spain, within a morning's car drive of Cadiz. Until it was destroyed by Carthage, about 500 B.C., Tartessus was the great market and bronze manufactory of the western world. Solomon's ships sailed to it. Greek merchants visited it. Until something is known about this famous city, students of

128

Bronze Age Britain are building a house on sand. We know that Irish gold and bronze work reached Spain. We know that glass beads and gold objects reached southern Britain from the eastern Mediterranean. What else happened? Irish gold rings have even been found in Palestine. I have shown elsewhere how the Irish skin-covered boat, the curragh, seems to be descended from a type still used, though built of wood, on the Portuguese coast today. The Turdetani of Tartessus also used skin boats.

The strong connection between Bronze Age Spain and the British Isles is clear enough. All the ancient chronicles, as well as archaeology, tell of it. And yet the great truth behind it all remains unsought. Tartessus had a written language which might tell us much.

Still I fancy that Bronze Age Britain was too united and had too highly organized a priesthood to be much affected by new beliefs, which did not conform to those already held. Beliefs like that in the transfer of souls in the Boat of the Dead might drift in here and there. Sir Cyril Fox found what was undoubtedly an example of this idea in a Welsh barrow. This also seems to be suggested by some Scandinavian rock engravings. Earlier than the general age of cremation in Britain, it was perhaps not incompatible with the earliest form of sun and moon worship. When cremation became universal, these ideas appear to have died out. A priesthood, which could enforce the removal of the Prescelly stone circle to Stonehenge, was not likely to tolerate much diversity of religious opinion.

With the deterioration of the climate in the late Bronze Age much trouble must have occurred. Very many of the people may have died throughout the land from famine and even war for food-producing lands. Into this as yet smudgy and uncertain picture, came the latest Bronze Age urnfielders and the earliest Iron Age Celts. At least three large immigrations of Celtic peoples arrived in the southern half of Britain; although it is still uncertain whether the latest wave of so-called Belgic tribes were Celticized Germans or Germanized Celts. It seems probable that the custom of making giant figures was in use before the Belgic migration began, somewhere about the year 100 B.C. Since the horses are of an Iron Age, rather than a Bronze Age, type, it is pretty clear that the Celtic immigrants were devotees of the same religion as the Bronze Age people; while the coins of the Belgic dynasty of Cunobelin, which lasted down to the Roman invasion, bear numerous representations of the horse and moon. They also sometimes have pictures of Ogmius with his club.

There is thus no evidence of any break in the ritual performance of this particular faith for over fifteen hundred years. If the witch cult is a part of it, as I think it is, the religion is still here to-day. Its superstitions certainly remain. Many other gods and goddesses joined the Celtic pantheon. Many more became temporary visitors in the days of the Roman Empire. Saxon and Norse deities arrived and faded out. The original beliefs of the earliest pastoral peoples outlasted the whole lot of them. It is a very remarkable story. In India nothing has been able to destroy this ancient faith. Relying on the assumption that there was no material break or change in the religion, it is reasonable to use the information we have collected about the Celtic and later phases of the cult and try to apply this to archaeological phenomena belonging to an earlier time.

I suppose we will all agree that the most interesting prehistoric monument in Britain is Stonehenge. This remarkable relic, known significantly enough to Geoffrey of Monmouth as the 'Giant's Dance', has caused more controversy than any other, and its purpose is still undecided. In the last few years I have seen it explained either as a glorified cattle pen, or a place for orgiastic dances. For years, following the suggestion of John Aubrey in the seventeenth century, it was universally hailed as a Druidic temple.[1] Others would see in it an elaborate astronomical instrument. John Wood of Bath suggested that it was a lunar temple for the worship of Diana. Sir Thomas Kendrick gave very impressive reasons for thinking that it really had been used as a Druidic temple; a view scouted by most archaeologists, who believing in an early Bronze Age date deduced from excavation results, could see no connection with a priesthood nearly a thousand years later. I am not concerned now with whether the priests of the Bronze Age, chiefs, or an organized religious body, were known as Druids or not. I do think, however, that it is possible to form a reasonable appreciation of the purpose for which Stonehenge was built, based on the investigations which we have already made. Stonehenge consists of two inner horseshoes of stones, within several outer rings of stones, pits and a

[1] Sir Thomas Kendrick summarizes the various theories of origin in *The Druids*.

ditch. The rings seem to me to demarcate the courses of Solar dances; the horseshoes, including the five enormous archways, known as trilithons, are connected with the moon. The 'Heel' stone is surely a stone of Helith the sun god. Perhaps the whole construction was once known as the Heel stones to local people. Whatever may be the truth of this, I feel reasonably certain that the purpose of the whole thing was the conducting of ritual and religious dances as the rites of both sun and moon alike. Whether Sir Thomas Kendrick's theory that the mortice and tenon method used in construction of the trilithons and the circular ring of capped stones can only have come from Classical sources in the Iron Age can now be held, I do not know. The discovery on the stones of pictures, supposed to be representations of Bronze Age axes and daggers, if not the result of a method of squaring the surface of the stones with chisels of some kind, may be thought to outweigh the evidence of the tenons. I do not think it affects our quest to any extent. Sir Thomas was clearly right in believing that the place was used for Druidic rites. The long 'cursus', or avenue, leading to it, presumably marked the route of a processional approach. The use of an astronomical layout appears to be correct and in keeping with the contemporary reports of the astrological activities of the Druidic priesthood. Exactly what went on there will never be known; but if victims were sacrificed, they would have been burnt and great heaps of ashes noted in the excavations. Beltane was the great time for burning people; Stonehenge was apparently used for a midsummer and midwinter festival. That tends to make the monument later than the truly pastoral age and after the general introduction of agriculture on a large scale. Stonehenge was, in fact, a religious site, which, like a medieval church, was constantly being changed and added to. The earliest date of its construction has little bearing on the date of the latest additions. I have not the slightest doubt that, as Sir Thomas said, it was in use during the Celtic Iron Age and the succeeding Roman Period. Occasional ceremonies may have taken place there down to very much later times.

I return once more to the question of the Druids. Their name is certainly connected with the Celtic root 'dru' for oak. They were reported by contemporaries as priests of the sacred oak in the sacred grove. The oak was the tree of the sun god. If, therefore, we can show early examples of the use of the sacred groves, or rites connected with the oak, it will go a long way to show that a priesthood of Druidic type existed in Britain before the Iron Age Celts arrived. These Celts may have been the first to call them Druids, but they would have been Druids none the less. 'A rose, by any other name, would smell as sweet.' I do not, of course, know what the Druids smelt like; but you can see what I mean.

Now in the last twenty-five years or so there have been several discoveries of timber circles. The two best-known being the site known as 'Woodhenge' near Stonehenge itself and Arminghall in East Anglia. This latter site is said to be connected with a story of a giant, but I do not know the details. The finds of objects within these circles show that they are at least as early as the earliest circles at Stonehenge and probably preceded its erection. The circles consist of several concentric rings of post-holes. At Woodhenge an infant had apparently been killed and buried in the centre as a foundation sacrifice. These circles must surely be artificially constructed sacred oak groves. There seems to be no other reasonable explanation. It is widely thought that Woodhenge was an ancestral Stonehenge. The lintels at Stonehenge may well have been intended as symbolic branches of trees. Here then are your artificial oak groves. There are various other sanctuaries whose rings of post-holes suggest another form of the same idea.

There is another pointer in the same direction. Occasionally in Britain and more frequently in Denmark human bodies are found buried in what are known as 'oak coffins'. These are not coffins in the ordinary sense; but are large sections of tree trunks, split lengthwise and hollowed out to contain the body. This was a work of such apparently unnecessary labour that one can only feel that the idea was to make the person, buried in the trunk, at one with the oak tree itself and as such at one with the sun itself. The only persons for whom, one feels, such an undertaking would have been carried out are priests or priestesses of the sacred grove.[1] In the Gristhorpe barrow near Scarborough,

[1] I have often wondered whether the gruesome story of the bride accidentally shut up in an oak chest and not found for many years is not a legendary memory of some such practice. The story is attached to many old houses, which shows that the original site of the happening is forgotten. It is always known as 'The Mitletoe Bough' for no reason connected with the tale.

opened in A.D. 1834, the skeleton of an old man, accompanied by a bronze dagger and flint implements, was buried in an oak coffin covered with oak branches. It was thought at the time that there was evidence for the remains of mistletoe in the coffin. This is now less certain.[1] It seems most probable that this was a Bronze Age priest of the sun. He may also have been a chieftain. To call him a Druid is perhaps an anachronism; but apparently he was one in practice. This archaeological evidence is of great importance, for it points to the existence of the Druidic worship in Britain long before the coming of the Iron Age Celts. It also shows that the religion, which was almost universal in Britain throughout the Bronze Age was Druidic. This seems to me to be a conclusive argument that the Iron Age Celts did not introduce Druidism in Britain.

The so-called 'Pictish' stone carvings are one of the most interesting series of antiquities in Britain. There are a large number of these, mostly carved on upright monoliths. They are found in all the areas of Scotland, which are supposed to have formed the kingdom of the Picts; from the central lowlands of Scotland right round to the Outer Hebrides. The thickest distribution, however, is in the east and north-east. The carvings date from the post-Roman period. This dating is secured by the fact that very many of the carvings carry interlacing ribbon patterns on them, which can be compared with similar patterns on the well-known illuminated Christian manuscript books, such as Durrow, Kells and Lindisfarne. The exact dating of the series of Pictish stones is still a debatable matter; but it is reasonable to suppose that they are not earlier than the seventh century of our era. Opinions still differ as to whether they started with elaborate examples and degenerated into simpler forms or whether the reverse process took place. As a general rule in this country, art forms appear to start with simple ideas, suddenly develop to highly ornate forms and then fade away again.

The great interest in these Pictish carvings lies in the symbols which form part of the design. Although they are often found on the same stone as undoubtedly Christian symbols, particularly the Cross, there seems little doubt that they are in themselves pagan. Cormac's glossary states that the pagans cut

---

[1] For an appreciation, see T. D. Kendrick, *The Druids*, p. 124.

the symbols of their gods on stones and mentions that of the sun as an example.

Sickle moons are probably the most numerous. I have made no statistical survey, and this is only an impression. Then there are circles with central dots, which if found on Bronze Age objects would be called 'sun discs'; combs and mirrors also are found carved on the stones. Then there are numerous representations of animals, some of which have degenerated into monstrosties. These certainly remained in use on Christian crosses down to the ninth century if not later. The most common animals are the horse, a horned deer, bull, boar, serpent, fish, eagle and hound. It might be claimed that the fish is a Christian symbol, were it not also a symbol of Astarte. A broken rod, which often passes through the moon symbol, may perhaps be taken for an indication of death. The animals seem undoubtedly to be cult animals. Some apparently survive to this day in the arms of leading families.

Of these animals the horse, the horned deer, the bull, boar, serpent and the fish are all associated with a moon goddess in one form or another. Perhaps it would be more accurate to associate the bull with the sun, but there is no close distinction. Baal started as female and became male. At any rate the horse and the horned deer were directly associated with Diana and also Artemis. The boar was associated with Artemis and the Highland Cailleach. Hence the Scottish taboo on eating pork. The fish was a symbol of Astarte; the bull and serpent of the sun god Taranis or Jupiter.

It looks very much as if the Picts were making the most of two religions; just as the ancient Hebrews appear to have believed in the existence of Baal as well as Jehovah. When we find a Christian cross deliberately cut on top of these apparently pagan symbols it looks like evidence of ecclesiastical disapproval (Fig. 15).

Now there are several interesting points to be noticed. First, the Pictish area is one which is very rich in evidence for the former existence of the sun and moon cult. Stone circles and cup marked stones, often associated together, are found all over it. Secondly, among the Picts, the descent of rule through the female line remained the custom far down into historic times and was probably not finally crushed before the tenth century

Fig. 15—Various symbols sketched from 'Pictish' carved stones. Hound, Cailleach's Boar, Horse, Bird, Deer, Two combs, Snakes, Sun disc, Lunar Symbol and mirror which may be a lunar symbol also.

after Christ. Dr. T. T. Paterson believes that he can see traces of mother rule among the people of Fife today. Thirdly, this was an area in which the Christian church had a prolonged struggle and the greatest difficulty in putting down the covens of witches.[1] James I of England went about in dread of the witches and wrote a book denouncing them. Coming from that part of the world, he evidently believed strongly in their power. Lastly, the Romans never succeeded in conquering this part of Scotland. Druids were neither suppressed, nor exterminated.

It is not unexpected to find evidence for the existence of two beliefs side by side and in the same individual. Not only is there the Biblical testimony for it among the ancient Hebrews; but, if Dr. Margaret Murray is right, which I feel sure is the case, the ruling families of England, down to Plantagenet times, were devotees of both religions.

To say, 'This is a monument erected in Christian times and therefore the symbolism on it must be Christian,' is an unrealistic approach. The rites of the older faith, now regarded as superstition, are practised all over the country to-day. It did not mean that people were not Christian; but that they could see a lot of sense in the old beliefs also. The idea of transmigration and subsequent rebirth on earth, may well have had a wider appeal to Celtic warriors, than that of twanging a harp in the sky, or resting on the bosom of Abraham. It will be remembered too that a wise instruction to the clergy had said that where pagan customs were found too strong to be easily eliminated, they were to be moulded into the semblance of Christianity. Many of the rites of Isis became Christian ceremonies; many pagan gods and goddesses were canonized as Christian saints; Brigid became St. Bridget, Ma and Matrona became Mary. In this manner much dangerous opposition was muzzled and the way prepared for the slow decay of paganism. Where people had been in the habit of making human sacrifices for the general good, they found that they need not do so any more, because of the sacrifice of Christ. The sacrifice of the Son of God Himself was at once understood as being intended to relieve people of this tax for ever. They did not, however,

---

[1] In the Highlands of Scotland and in Ireland, witches were not organized in covens. There is a distinction between a single witch and the group.

necessarily believe that the sun and moon had lost their importance. The sun still made things grow; the moon still gave her
light; the demon of darkness was yet there as the Devil. Presumably the sun and moon had still their attributes, so 'put
them on the stone for luck'. The popularity of the wheel cross
among the Celtic peoples may well be due to its resemblance
to a sun disc. On the most beautiful crosses in the west of
Scotland, not only is there the solar dischead; but there are also
domed bosses, which may well have been intended to represent
lunar symbols. All three elements are there, the cross, the sun
and the moon. No wonder they were popular. Gaels used to
swear by sun and moon.

A similar problem to that of the Pictish stones is related to
another series of carvings, which are also found in a Christian
context. On the walls of many churches in England, Scotland
and Ireland, grossly indecent carvings of the female figure are
to be seen. In Ireland they are sometimes found on castles.
Many more probably exist than have been actually noted. Some
years ago the term, anglicized as Shiela-na-Gig, was found in
use for one of them and has now become the technical term for
the whole group. Although some of the stones may be older
than the buildings on which they are now found, there appear
to be few cases of their occurrence on a building older than the
eleventh century and they are sometimes clearly contemporary
with the actual construction. The most isolated example known
is that on the church tower at Rodel in Harris, on the far side
of the Minch. The tower on which it is to be seen is evidently
of late medieval date, but the stone appears to be older.

The name Shiela-na-Gig has proved difficult to explain.
Those who would see the word 'cioch' a breast as an explanation for 'gig', have to explain why the breasts are seldom
emphasized on these figures. It is, however, not so difficult if
Harold Bayley's view is accepted and we take 'gig' as no more
than a variant of 'gog'.[1] The name Shiela-na-Gig would then
translate with little difficulty as 'the holy lady of Gog'. That
is 'Magog', or Maha-devi, Holy Maha.

This seems a surprising identification, but it is less surprising
than the occurrence of numerous examples of such things on
church building at so late a date. It must be taken in conjunction

---

[1] Harold Bayley, *Archaic England*, p. 194.

Fig. 16a—Group of ? Medieval carvings from the 'Royston Cave'. Although some of the groups in this unexplained artificial cave are clearly Christian, others including this one appear to be pagan. The sword, indicating a cross, can be a Christian symbol, but is also carried by Astarte. The horse, shiela-na-gig figure and sun disc are evidently pagan. The whole group appears to be contemporary. Astarte in later times seems to have become St. Margaret.

Fig. 16b—Etruscan Mother-Goddess of 'Cailleach' type, holding off two lionesses.

with the discovery of obscene objects beneath the altars of some Welsh churches.

Dr. Margaret Murray has cited instances of Christian priests being accused of taking part in 'Devil' worship. In A.D. 1282 the priest of Inverkeithing led a fertility dance at Easter round a phallic figure of a god. In A.D. 1303 the Bishop of Coventry, Lady Godiva's city, was accused before the Pope of doing homage to the Devil.

That the religion was still strong in England in the eleventh century is clear from Canute's law on the subject, which runs as follows:[1] 'We earnestly forbid every heathenism: heathenism is that men worship idols; that is, that they worship heathen gods, and the sun or moon, fire or rivers, water-wells or stones, or forest trees of any kind; or love witchcraft or promote morthwork of any wise.'

It is evident then that four hundred years of Christianity had not displaced the old religions. The church too had continual difficulty in preventing the eating of sacrificial horses. In the end it established a taboo against eating horse-flesh at all in Britain; but it was a hard struggle.

If Dr. Murray is right, the Norman kings, down to the Plantagenets, were devotees of the witch cult. They were at the same time fulfilling the rites of the church. Presumably they held some of the beliefs of both religions and saw nothing inconsistent in doing so: neither, apparently, did the priests. It is not, therefore, as strange as anyone might think to find evidence for fertility cult on a church building. Several of the carvings found on churches and one of the objects, a bronze casting, found beneath an altar, evidently were intended to represent the sacred marriage of sun and moon; or sun and the great Earth Mother. The rest represent the Great Mother only, prepared for that marriage.

As I said once before some years ago in *Merlin's Island*, if you have a theory which is wrong, you find many things which will not fit into it. If, however, you have one which is right, very many things, which you never thought of, drop into place. In this particular study, the confirmation of the theory has come from many unexpected places and nothing has as yet turned up to make me doubt that the theory is correct. Any research of

[1] Benjamin Thorpe, *Monumenta Ecclesiastica*, vol. 1, p. 379.

this kind can never be more than theory. It is only when theory becomes dogma and is taught in schools as truth, that it becomes a menace to further investigation.

If my ideas about the long life and widespread significance of sun and moon worship are correct, it should be possible to see some traces of it in the small objects in use in everyday life. Here I shall deliberately avoid the numerous dedicatory inscriptions to a host of gods made during the Roman Period. This could be followed up at some other time. My object will be to see particularly whether there is any reflection of the religion in other ages and cultures. To see what I am attempting to do, it is only necessary to turn up the British Museum Guide to Medieval Antiquities (1924). On page 12 is a figure of a fine medieval sword dredged from the river Witham. On the blade beside the inscription and a symbol of the cross there are also two sun symbols, four moon symbols and two other symbols whose meaning I do not know. These are charms. On page 258 is a rather fantastically shaped pastry-cook's knife, with a sickle lunar blade for cutting and a solar wheel for marking the pastry. There was no apparent need for it to have been this shape, but students of the Bible will remember the rite of making 'moon-shaped' cakes. On page 271 there is a plate (Fig. 180) showing a pilgrim's badge. This was the sign that the wearer had been to the shrine of Thomas à Becket. The badge is an obvious sun disc with the martyr's head in the middle. But Dr. Murray has given good reason for thinking that Becket was a sacrificial victim of the witch cult. This kind of thing could be followed up at length. Some identifications might be wrong, but there is enough to show that many are probably right.

Let us go back some distance in time, to a period on which I have done a great deal of work. Few people were greatly interested in the pagan Anglo-Saxons when I first became involved in excavating their graves thirty years ago. Since then I have had to deal with half a dozen cemeteries and several hundreds of graves. One of these cemeteries, the cremation cemetery at Lackford in Suffolk, involved the removal of about five hundred burial urns. Many of these were ornamented with stamped designs and a few had drawings on them. In an attempt to discover how far the products of one particular potter travelled, in say A.D. 550, I made a close study of the stamps found on pots, not only from the Lackford cemetery, but many others as well. I was not concerned with the character of the stamps, so much as with the possibility of recognizing the same stamp again in another place. As a matter of interest, pots appear to have been distributed over a distance of not less than twenty miles.

Now a place on which you naturally wish to have some kind of protective charm is a vessel in which you store perishable food, milk in particular. These Anglo-Saxon burial urns, in common with most cremation urns of all periods, are ordinary domestic vessels. They were seldom, or never, specially made for the occasion. It might be thought therefore that, although many of the stamps found on them might be mere ornament, or to stop the pot slipping out of greasy hands, some might well be charms. I therefore looked through my figures of stamps from Lackford.[1] If I have counted them correctly, there are two hundred and fifty different stamps. Of these eighty-seven would have been taken for sun discs, if they had been found engraved on rocks. They probably are sun discs, for it is not very easy to cut a ring and dot stamp on a piece of bone or stick. Some have more than one ring and others have toothing resembling rays (Fig. 17). One has a face indicated on it. Five are certainly swastikas, which I have not included in the eighty-seven total. The swastika is known to be a sun symbol. Thus more than a third of the total number of stamps appear to be sun charms.

As far as I can judge, twenty-one symbols are either cups, which again would be taken for moon symbols in another context, or stamps resembling crescent moons. While another three are definite horseshoes (Fig. 17). There are thirteen equal-armed crosses, which might either be Christian or sun symbols, and two 'Tau' crosses, which may have no significance. There are eighteen examples of S or serpent stamps, which are probably sun symbols, but may be lunar, one case of large incised serpents with eyes and two cases of serpents crossed to form swastikas. The remaining stamps are mainly squares or diamonds and probably just ornament, but there are some symbols which look like combs. In twelve instances the

[1] T. C. Lethbridge, 'A Cemetery at Lackford, Suffolk', *Cambridge Antiquarian Society Quarto Publications*, no. vi, 1951.

stamps, which I take to be sun and moon symbols, occur on the same pot. In one case the stamp of a whippet is found together with a swastika. This is probably a late pot and we are reminded of the hounds on the Pictish stones. There are, in fact, few

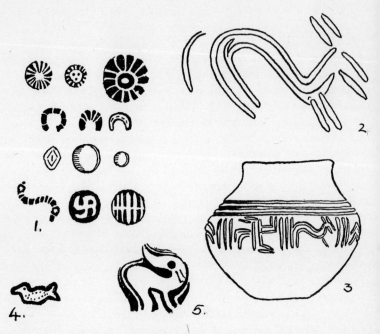

Fig. 17—1. Stamps on Anglo-Saxon pottery; sun-discs; horseshoes; moon symbols; snake, swastik and comb symbols. 2. Figure of a horse scratched on an Anglo-Saxon pot. 3. Anglo-Saxon pot with swastika and horse scratched on it. 4. Bird stamp. 5. Hound stamp.

No. 2 is 3 inches long; all others to same scale except No. 3 which is 6 inches high. All from the Lackford Cemetery, Suffolk. A similar collection of symbols is found on the 'Pictish' carved stones.

stamps on Anglo-Saxon pots which cannot be matched with Pictish symbols in Scotland.

Thus, from a study of the pot stamps alone, it would be possible to conclude that the sun and moon and their attendant animals were regarded as at any rate lucky by the mixed people, whom we know as Anglo-Saxons. There is, however, more to it than this. Eight pots from Lackford are ornamented with big domed bosses, pushed up from the inside, which can hardly be meant to represent anything other than breasts. These breasts are so common in Germany before the Anglo-Saxon Settlement

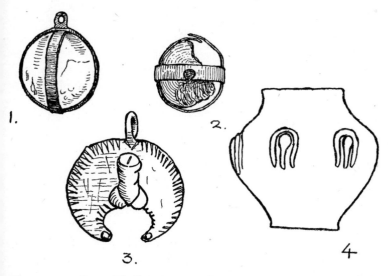

Fig. 18—1. Crystal ball in bronze slings. Burwell, Cambridgeshire (1¼ in. diameter). Anglo-Saxon, seventh century. 2. Oak-bark ball. Little Wilbraham. Anglo-Saxon, sixth century. 3. Lunar horseshoe phallic pendant. Guilden Morden. Romano-British, *c.* third century. Compare with modern horse-brasses and horseshoes hung up on nails. All to one scale. 4. Pagan Anglo-Saxon pot embossed with 'horseshoe and peg' ornament. This type of ornament was found on four pots in the cemetery at Lackford, Suffolk. This particular vessel is 8½ in. high and can be dated by its contents to about the middle of the sixth century.

of Britain, and right back to the Bronze Age in Central Europe, that we must feel that their intention is more ritualistic than ornamental. They are probably the breasts of the Mother Earth. (Baldwin Brown, *The Arts in Early England*, vol. 4, Pl. cxxxii, shows a pot of this type with the goddess's head as well as the breasts. This makes the identification reasonably clear.) There are also many pots in which these bosses are no longer circular and which cannot therefore be included. One may be phallic.

Together with these bossed pots, there are three of another type, also common on the Continent. Here a large, and often pointed boss, is surmounted by a raised, sausage-like horseshoe. This seems to be the 'horseshoe on a peg' symbol (Fig. 18). Other evidence of the importance of horses in connection with these pots, is given by the use of a pony's tooth as a stamp on one vessel and rough drawings of horses scratched on the clay of two others. On one of these, a single horse pairs a large swastika drawn beside it (Fig. 17). The swastika being a sun symbol, the horse is almost certainly a moon symbol also. On a pot in the Norwich Museum, Mr. Rainbird Clarke has observed a drawing of a war galley, emblem of the goddess whom Tacitus identified as Isis.

It seems to me therefore, although in many years of handling Anglo-Saxon pots it had not struck me before I began this inquiry, that there is ample evidence for some kind of veneration of the sun and moon by the Anglo-Saxons. Although Tacitus only mentions their sacred white horses, the worship of Nerthus (Mother Earth) and Isis's war-galley, there is proof in the presence of the swastikas that the sun came into the picture also. Although other gods were important, their emblems were not often applied to household goods. Here, however, the Tau cross could perhaps be taken for the symbol, which later became the 'Hammer of Thor'. A serpent, which occurs both here and on the Pictish symbol stones, is also known as an attribute of Jupiter-Taranis and so of the sun, it is also, however, frequently associated with moon and Mother Goddesses.

Perhaps this idea also explains a phenomenon, which can be noticed on the bulk of the Anglo-Saxon brooches. A very large proportion of these, the cruciform brooches, have a horse's head at one end. Others, known as square-headed and saucer brooches, have a human head, which resembles the head of Sul from the tymphanum of the Sul-Minerva temple at Bath (Fig. 19). Out of sixty-six brooches, which I found in the Anglo-Saxon cemetery of Holywell Row, Suffolk, eighteen had horse's heads on them, while only one had what I take to be a sun face. These were all worn by women. Horse's heads are also common on combs and not rare on buckles.

In Anglo-Saxon graves spheres, ground out of clear rock crystal and rather more than an inch in diameter, are found from

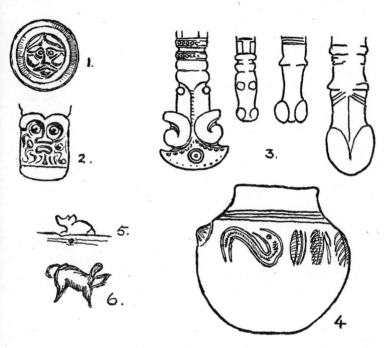

Fig. 19—Pagan Anglo-Saxon objects. 1. Sun disc brooch. Anglo-Saxon period after Baldwin Brown. Diameter *c.* 1 in. 2. Supposed Sun face from 'squareheaded' brooch. 3. Horse's heads from 'cruciform' brooches. These are typical of hundreds of examples. The one on the left appears to have lunar crescent and sun disc added beneath the nostrils. 4. Anglo-Saxon pot 8 2/5ths in. high, engraved with a serpent. 5. Anglo-Saxon boar carved on the back of a comb. 6. Anglo-Saxon boar engraved on a sword blade from the river Lark. (All to the same scale except No. 4 and all taken from my own reports except No. 1.)

time to time. They are slung in two hoops of wire, or bands of metal, which have a loop for suspension fastened to one of the points where they cross at right angles. These objects would be quite inexplicable were it not for the fact that several similar spheres have been preserved for long ages in some families in the Highlands of Scotland. One of these has been for centuries in the possession of the Stewarts of Ardvorlich on Loch Earn. This ball was always known as the 'Clach Dearg'—the Red Stone, although it is made of clear white crystal. When dipped in water this was given as a drink to cure sick cattle. This suggests that either the white ball was dipped in water which had some red substance in solution, or that it was coated with some soluble red material previously, and that this red material proved healthful to the cattle.

Now it happens that in 1926 I recovered a similar ball from an Anglo-Saxon grave at Little Wilbraham in Cambridgeshire, but this ball was made either of oak bark or possibly from an oak-gall of the 'oak apple' type. Tannin from oak bark or oak galls was formerly used as a cure for dysentery as may be seen in Culpepper's Herbal. It seems probable that the purpose of all these spheres is for both magical and herbal healing. The sphere represents the moon and the tannin does the work. The Christian Alemanni on the Upper Rhine sometimes carried little spherical boxes of silver or oak wood probably for the same purpose. In some Kentish graves the pendant sphere is accompanied by a large silver spoon perforated with holes for use as a strainer, which was no doubt used to extract chips of bark from the tannin-stained water. My oak bark ball was provided with a Roman folding bronze spoon. A crystal ball, which I found in a seventh century grave at Burwell had no spoon with it. Each had been worn suspended from a woman's girdle.

A crystal charm belonging to the MacDonell's of Keppoch, had to be dipped in water from a spring dedicated to Brigid. There seems little doubt that all were connected with a goddess and their shape suggests that this goddess was a lunar one.

Since I do not for a moment believe in any universal destruction, or general displacement of the rural population of Britain by the Anglo-Saxons; it is easy to see how the mixed race, which resulted from their settlement, would have continued the

festivals at Wandlebury, Cerne, Tysoe, Uffington and elsewhere. Such a population, in which all elements had apparently
venerated the same gods, would tend to crowd out such deities
as they did not have in common. It makes it easier to understand
how these Shiela-na-Gigs could not be omitted from the
churches.

The archaeology of Roman Britain is so full of traces of
worship of every kind of god and goddess, that it would be
waste of time to wade through the evidence here. Three
instances, bearing on our particular study, must be enough.

When Sir Cyril Fox and I excavated the Romano-British
cemetery at Guilden Morden, Cambridgeshire, the skeleton of
a man was found extended in a grave cut in the chalk. Very many
inhumations have been found here as well as cremations. The
majority of the graves with skeletons in them probably belong
to the second half of the Roman period; although I have found
men with Belgic grave goods. In a recess, cut in the wall of the
grave I have mentioned, lay an unusual collection of objects.
These were an iron ferrule, like one off a walking-stick, and a
bronze cylinder of approximately the same size. From one end
of this cylinder protruded a number of rusted links of fine iron
chain. From the chain had been suspended a bronze lunar
pendant; it was flat and slightly smaller than a horse brass.
On one side of the pendant and cast in one piece with it in the
mould, was a large phallus (Fig. 18). This pendant is the
ancestral form of the 'horseshoe and peg' symbol found on the
Anglo-Saxon pots mentioned on page 144 and of the horseshoes
placed in a similar way above many doorways today. It was
clear that the whole collection had formed one object. The head
of a staff had been tipped with a bronze collar and the phallic
pendant dangled from it on a short length of chain. The sides
of the cylinder were battered and covered with dents, where the
pendant had banged against them. The thing, not altogether
unlike a Fool's Bauble, must have belonged to somebody who
engaged in stimulating the populace at orgiastic festivities connected with the moon. Perhaps we might call him a priest of
Magog.[1] He also had an iron thumb-ring.

The second instance consists of the discovery of two boar's
tusks in the excavations at the Saxon Shore fort of Richborough.

[1] *Cambridge Antiquarian Society Proceedings*, vol. xxvi, p. 60, Fig. 6.

Each now consists of a single tusk in a metal holder at the hollow end. In each case there were at one time two tusks. They were halves of two lunar charms, such as were common until recently in the Balkans. A single boar's tusk, with a small hole in the hollow end, which I found in an Anglo-Saxon hut at Waterbeach in 1926, may have formed part of a similar pendant.

The third example links us with Hiccathrift. Many years ago, an important find of bronze cult objects was made in the Fens at a place called the Hempstalls, not far from the large and presumably Early Iron Age fort of Belsar's Hills at Willingham. The objects must have once belonged to some shrine, probably a public one and may have been deliberately concealed, like many other votive bronze figures found in the area, at the coming of Christianity. Amongst Hempsall's bronzes were two small statuettes of mounted soldiers in armour and a sceptre or baton of unusual form. The object has attracted the attention of many scholars, both British and Continental.[1] The figures on this baton are usually identified with Jupiter-Taranis. If this identification is correct, then the figure with the wheel who is thought to be fighting a giant is Taranis and thus Hiccathrift.

It is interesting too to note that statuettes of Hercules, with club and cloak, are relatively common in the district along with larger busts of Hercules, whose face is thought to be modelled on the head of the Emperor Commodus. Professor Heichelheim sees the two little figures of warriors on horses as Taranis fighting a giant and connected them with Gervase of Tilbury's tale of the Wandlebury figures.

These small and unspectacular discoveries are often of more importance than statues, or altars, for they point to the beliefs of ordinary people and not to wealthy magistrates or governors. We should not, however, forget the ferocious sun god from Bath. He is Gog, or Ogma Sunface, without much doubt; for he is the Sul of Aquae Sulis and his mother was Minerva.[2]

Owing to the extremely developed art styles of the Celtic Iron Age, it is not easy to pick out religious symbols. Some, however, certainly exist. The well-known bronze-mounted bucket from Aylesford, Kent, which was presumably intended

---

[1] E.g., Professor F. Heichelheim, *Cambridge Antiquarian Society Proceedings*, vol. xxxvii. [2] Sir Thomas Kendrick, *Anglo-Saxon Art*, Methuen 1938, Pl. vi.

for a milk pail, might be expected to carry some protective charms (see British Museum Early Iron Age Guide, 1925, Fig. 135). In fact it appears to do so. Sun discs alternate with pairs of horses round its rim; while the human heads on the handle have lunar head-dresses. Similar protective charms are found on buckets and bowls right down to the Viking Age (see British Museum Anglo-Saxon Guide, 1923, Fig. 127).[1] A sun disc wheel from Hounslow and a moon goddess statuette from Aust-on-Severn are also quite obvious (Early Iron Age Guide, Figs. 172 and 173). Charms, however, do not seem to be found on our English Iron Age pottery vessels; although they do occur occasionally on Continental pots. A good example of a horse drawn on the clay of a pot, before it was fired, is shown in Paul Jacobsthal's *Early Celtic Art*, Plate 208, No. 410.

A considerable mass of pottery of what must be considered Iron Age culture, though of Roman date, has now been recovered from brochs and wheel-houses in the Hebrides. The bulk of the ornamented pottery is simply slashed, or grooved, with geometric patterns. A few pieces, however, have been found bearing stamped decoration. Those found up to now are ring-shaped rosettes, which might be thought to be sun symbols, or broken circles of nearly horseshoe form, made by pressing the ring of a wire pin into the clay. It might be unwise even to think of these as being sun and moon charms, were it not for the fact that the only two examples of pottery engraved with free-hand drawings, one of which I found myself, are ornamented with horned deer.[2] It seems quite probable that we have in the Hebrides the same idea that we noted on the Anglo-Saxon pottery. In any case, it is worth bearing this in mind. A knuckle-bone from the broch of Burrian in Orkney was found with 'Pictish' symbols scratched on it. It seems to have been from a later level than the original occupation of the broch. I have no doubt that more examples could easily be recognized on objects of the Celtic Iron Age, but it is unnecessary to do so now.

In the Bronze Age we have so many conspicuous traces of this religion, that it is not necessary to labour the point. On smaller things there is not much to help us in Britain; although there is much of it in Denmark. The only objects, which occur

[1] T. C. Lethbridge, *Anthropological Journal*, vol. 83, part 2, p. 175.
[2] T. C. Lethbridge, *The Painted Men*, Andrew Melrose, 1954, Fig. 10.

readily to my mind, are the large pottery vessels known as 'encrusted urns'.[1] Some of these may well be thought to carry solar and lunar symbols.

This brief survey, covering nearly three thousand years, is enough to show that sun and moon charms may be found at almost any period and scattered too all over the land. It is just the same on the Continent. Sun and moon were evidently regarded as most potent factors in daily life.

[1] E.g., Professor Grahame Clark, *Prehistoric England*, Batsford 1940, Fig. 13.

Chapter Nine

DRUIDISM was only one of many religions in Gaul and not necessarily the most widespread. Caesar tells us that Mercury was the Gaulish god to whom most reverence was paid and who had the most statues.

Now by saying Mercury, Caesar was equating him with a group of three Gaulish gods, all of which had some of the attributes of Mercury.[1] They were Teutates, Esus and Taranis. Tautates and Esus both shared the qualities of Mercury and Mars. Esus sounds remarkably like Zeus and was shown by a tree. Teutates was the god to whom victims were given by drowning them head-downwards in a tub of water. A picture of this rite being performed, to the accompaniment of the blowing of horns, is shown on the famous Gundestrup silver bowl (Fig. 20b). The difficulty with all this is that there were so many names for each god. The same is true of Indian deities today. Siva has many names and so has Maha-devi.

Robert Graves[2] is clearly right in postulating a triple phase in the personalities of many ancient gods and goddesses. They might be young, in the prime of life, or old. Thus there were many groups of three Mother Goddesses, known to the Romans as Matronae, sometimes with moon haloes on their heads. These seem to be three phases of our Magog, or Mother Earth, or Moon Goddess. All these phases were known by different names: each phase also had many names in different localities. The difficulty of deciding whether one particular god or goddess is the same as another is very great.

It is quite clear, however, that Teutates, Esus and Taranis may well belong to our Gog and Magog series. There is no

[1] See Mrs. Olwen Brogan, *Roman Gaul*, Bell 1953.
[2] Robert Graves, *The Greek Myths*, Penguin.

reason to suppose that their priests were not Druids. That they were revered in Britain is shown by an inscription at Chester to Jupiter-Taranis. He was associated with sun-wheel, bull and serpent attributes. These were the most important gods in Gaul and probably important gods in Britain. At the same time contemporary writers say that the Gaulish Druids went over to Britain to learn their religion in its purest form. From this we must infer that the Druidic religion was not necessarily an

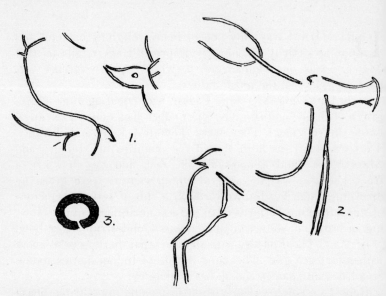

Fig. 20a—1. Deer scratched on potsherd from a South Uist Wheel-house at Kilpheder (2¼ in. overall length). 2. Deer scratched on potsherds from Coll (after Beveridge). 3. Horseshoe stamp made by a metal pin-head. This type of stamping is found from the Orkneys to Barra. Examples of sun-disc stamps are rare and too small for illustration. (All to the same scale.)

import into Britain by the Celtic Iron Age peoples. In Gaul it was probably confined to some of their tribes and much mixed with the worship of other gods; or restricted to different strata in their society.

The Celts had pushed into Gaul over the Rhine from districts which became German and were German lands in the days of

Caesar and Tacitus. Caesar tells us that the Germans had no Druids. Yet we have seen something which is much like a weak survival of part of the religion in the worship of the Earth Mother, Nerthus and her perigrinations with her priest. He might be thought to represent her original husband. In Scandinavia, in post-Roman times, a similar ritual was performed, in which an image of Frey was taken round the country in a wagon with a young priestess beside him, as his bride with the title of wife.

Fig. 20b—Sketches of representations of Celtic Gods drawn from the figures on the Gundestrup bowl. These are just sketches of embossed work and cannot be exact. The bowl is thought to have been imported into Jutland from central Europe between 200 B.C. and the Birth of Christ. 1. Cernunnos, holding 'lunar' torque. 2. Sacrifice to Teutates.

Here, with the change from rule by women to that by men, the chief figure is that of a god and not a goddess. It is interesting to note that a kind of horse worship has been traced in connection with Frey, or Ingvi as he seems to be called at one time.[1] It is believed that Skirnir, the Shining One, was originally a name for Frey. The resemblance to the epithet for Siva is suggestive.

Frey was not one of the higher kind of the gods of the north. It seems that he was a popular god, as opposed to those of the warrior caste, being more or less concerned only with fertility.

[1] For an account of Scandinavian religions, P. A. Munch, *Norse Mythology* Oxford 1926, is as good as any.

It appears from recent studies by physical anthropologists that there was a stratum in the old Norse population, which closely resembled the physical types found in the west of the British Isles and the inference is that an earlier population was overrun by invaders, of what we now regard as the tall, fair-haired Norse type, from more southern lands. In fact, the Bronze Age population of Scandinavia was probably closely allied to that of the British Isles, while the Viking invaders of our land were led by men of a different race. Frey worship, then, may well have been a debased version of our Gog and Magog religion.

It seems then that though this religion had once been widespread, by the time of Caesar it had been largely overshadowed by that of other gods, except in parts of Gaul and in the British Isles. In the British Isles it had been so strong in the Bronze Age and the priesthood so highly developed that it held its own against such worship of other gods as was imported later. The number of earliest Iron Age immigrants here seems to have been comparatively small and in eastern England at any rate Bronze Age influence in the styles of pottery forms suggests a rapid mingling of populations.

What I have written in this book should serve as a terrible warning to those who lightheartedly embark on a search for giants. A problem, which did not seem of any great moment to me, has plunged me into months of fieldwork, blistered hands, scratched ears and rheumatic joints. It has led me also far down paths of investigation, which I had never intended to tread. The archaeology was mostly in my head already and so were Dr. Murray's books on witches, Frazer's *Golden Bough*, Ridgeway's *Early Age of Greece*, and Bayley's *Archaic England*. I had very little idea, however, of ever delving among the religions of the Near East, or India. But for a clue in Petrie's paper on the Hill Figures, I should never have gone that way. I see now that one might spend a lifetime on this kind of thing and still have more to do at the end of it. But it is worth doing, for it opens up a glimpse of the ideas of men in Europe long ago, which can scarcely be obtained from a study of the less developed races in Africa or the Pacific to-day. There is no means of telling how many garbled ideas may not have reached them and formed part of their beliefs. In chasing the old religions of Europe, we seem to be able to watch the spread in every direction of one great belief. It came on top of vague and scattered beliefs in some form of totemism. It was so much higher in the scale of ideas, that people jumped at it, as later they did at Christianity. Although the thoughts of many men probably went to form it, one suspects that only one really great thinker hammered it into shape.

In attempting to appreciate how this idea was thought out, we must remember the background from which it came. Men believed in some close relationship with animals. It is not necessary here to go deeply into the vexed question of totemism. It is enough to know that groups of men associated themselves closely with some particular animal, or even plant. It was a sin to kill it without permission. In some way, which is hard for us to understand, the particular animal of each totem group was one of themselves, whether it was a cow or a lobster. It was a potent aid to them in many ways. Whether an original belief in the transmigration of souls into the totem animals was at the back of this idea, I do not know. It is perhaps more probable that our hypothetical philosopher began with the totem idea in his mind. He was a member of a pastoral tribe of which some horned beast, probably a cow was the totem. Reasoning from what he believed, he came to the conclusion that after death the soul would pass into the totem animal, if it was worthy to do so and would then be born again in human form. But it was clear to him that quite a lot of his neighbours were not worthy of this future. Well, since he believed the soul to be indestructible, their souls must pass into some inferior animal. Probably they went into the totem animal of those barbarous swine in the next glen. They, of all things, had a snake totem. This, I think, is the answer to the origin of the doctrine of transmigration. It was the most important article of faith and remains so over much of the world today.

Coming from a pastoral community, the fertility of man and beast was a most vital consideration. Who was responsible for that? Two powers must be, for a father and mother were necessary for all procreation. The great heat- and light-giving bodies, which passed overhead, must always have impressed men with awe. One of them clearly showed the same feature which was observed in the horns of his totem animal. People had always noticed this. This must be the Great Mother. The sun then must be the Father. I have already drawn attention to the danger, which appeared to threaten these two life-givers, from the demon of darkness.

Here then, it seems, we may look at a relatively simple explanation for the whole thing. Tribe after tribe accepted this general belief and totem animal after totem animal was added. Thus we find different beasts associated with the moon goddess in different areas. For the same reason, we find different names for the goddess herself. They are the local names for the totem animal.

The rites and sacrifices began as sympathetic magic. They were no part of the philosophy. This probably contained the germs of the great mass of poetic lore which had to be remembered. The stronger the priestly class grew, the greater the number of rites and sacrifices would be. This is common to all priestly castes everywhere. The dogma, often absurd, becomes more important than the original teaching. It is so with every religion, for it enhances the importance of the priests and makes them indispensable.

Here I shall leave the quest for the moment. It has been most fascinating, and I think I have only reached a halting place on the road. Innumerable questions still keep tumbling into my mind. Was the Highland water-horse, for instance, only an idle tale of the imagination formed from vague stories of the hippopotamus in Egypt? Was it not rather a legend of former sacrifices to Isis, the moon goddess of the sea, coupled with Diana's horse, her totem horse? Similarly, what was the story behind the animal at Loch na Beiste, Skye? This, I have been told was traditionally a bull with one leg. Was this just a vagrant walrus from Greenland? Is it more likely that some bull-headed seagod, perhaps Shony, was once worshipped here? I do not know the answers to these and to many more questions. I have, however, seen that folk-lore, which at one time did not seem to me to be a very promising line of investigation, can be linked in with archaeology and anthropology to give us a clearer understanding of much that we do not know. The nebulous Gog and Magog of folk tales have become most concrete facts. I do not think that I have been wasting my time.

Now, after briefly describing some of the many reasons for thinking that the worship of the Earth Mother, the moon, and of her husband, son, or lover the sun was one of the most permanent beliefs in Britain, I shall try to estimate what appears to have formed one of the chief rituals in this worship. I am not concerned here with the human sacrifice side of the matter, which crops up again and again in folk-lore all over our islands. I am only trying to trace the ritual which seems to be portrayed in pictures at Wandlebury. Its performance was regarded as necessary to ensure the continual progress of the seasons, which had to be carried out in face of the opposition of the Powers of Darkness.

The ritual, I think, was this. In its simplest form, before the sun, as the male god, became of greater importance to the rulers of the land than the moon, the Great Earth Goddess, something had to be done to help the moon past the clutches of the Demon of Darkness, winter and scarcity. The moon, closely associated through totemism with the horse, deer, cow and other animals, was represented as an old woman riding on a white horse, who, after some ritual struggle, reappeared as a radiant young girl. That is why Godiva is veiled or blackened. At first she represented the old moon and then, after a struggle such as the traditional one in Kintyre, she reappeared as a new moon. In many parts of the old world, her father was a male god in human form and her mother was a mare. The mare was really the totem and has survived in many places long after its rider has faded into the mists. When, I think, as at Finchampstead, a ghost white horse passes up an ancient road on to the top of an isolated, breast-like hill, this is the very last remembrance of a ceremony resembling that of Godiva at Coventry. A woman painted black, or veiled in some way, used to ride in procession up that hill and was then revealed by the priests, after being washed or otherwise uncovered in some sacred grove or precinct on the top. Our hill-figures are simply more permanent examples of a different manner of portraying the same idea. They may not all represent the same myth, but that does not matter for the present. Later on it should be possible to work out what they all are.

It must be remembered, however, that there was a change in belief, which corresponded to the change from female rule and descent to that of the male. With this change the moon tended to assume second place to her husband the sun. This change, however, did not destroy popular belief in the greater importance of the moon. And so the belief in Magog, Godiva, Black Annis or the Cailleach remained long after solar rituals had become numerous and widespread. Both, however, are still with us in the form of superstition.

It was, I fancy, the Belgae who introduced the belief in the greater importance of the male gods, but the idea became more or less universal. Only the Picts held strongly to the old ways, just as in the eighteenth century they were ready to fight for the older Roman Catholic faith against a Protestant king. But, even in the south, people who had been overrun by Belgae, Romans, Saxons, Norsemen and Normans still held on to their belief in the importance of the Great Mother. Godiva still rides through the streets of Coventry; although all knowledge of why she does so is forgotten.

It seems certain that it was customary over a wide area to regard each deity as being a trinity and they are frequently shown with three faces. Janus, the Keeper of the Gates of Heaven, is a well-known example; although he is usually portrayed with two faces, at one time he had three. Gaulish gods in the Roman period were sometimes shown with three faces, although others of an earlier date are only represented with two. The Mother Goddesses, Matronae, are normally shown in groups of three. In other words, whatever the god or goddess happened to be called, he or she was at one time part of a trinity representing youth, middle age and age, corresponding to the three phases of the moon. As time went on these trinities broke down into single deities and in many places were worshipped in isolation. The original grouping at one time may have evolved from the family, father, mother and child, such as Osiris, Isis and Horus in Egypt. But its more probable origin appears to have been the phases of the moon in comparison with the human life circle. Our Gog and Magog were each once a member of a trinity and probably also members of a family group. By the time we find them here, Magog shows clear signs of her triple aspect, and Gog as Ogmius or Helith has three most definite phases.

If we once appreciate that we are not really looking for traces of many gods and goddesses, but only for phases of comparatively few deities with differing names, it must be possible to learn much more about them. There is, for instance, a great deal of recorded tradition concerning the Cailleach and her black and venomous boar or sow, her horse and her following of animals. A Hebridean dance was formerly performed at wakes symbolizing the dying year and reviving spring. The English title of this dance is 'The Carlin of the Mill Dust', but Carlin is only the translation of Cailleach. The 'Old Sow', or 'Devil', who takes the 'Hindmost', in the Welsh rush from the bonfire, is simply the Cailleach's venomous pig. The horrible Mari Llwyd, with its horse's skull, which used to burst into houses in South Wales about New Year's Eve, is the Cailleach's mare, as are the processional hobby-horses, hob-knobs, hoden-horses and the like found till recently from Kent to Cornwall and away throughout the country northwards.

The whole thing hangs together as one picture spread over a wide area of the old world and it is of very great antiquity. I feel quite certain that a pony's skull, which was found carefully buried in one of the group of Bronze Age barrows, which I excavated at Snailwell in Cambridgeshire, was a ritual burial belonging to the same story. It was probably not less than 3,300 years old.

As the sun became relatively more important than the moon, his figure, of greater size, was added and so we find both Gog and Magog together being aided by ritual performance to defeat Wandil, the demon of darkness. Sometimes, as in Scandinavia, the male god appears to have entirely ousted the female. Frey and his stallion took the place of Magog and her mare. Traces of the worship of the stallion's phallus have been traced as late as Saga times. But Frey himself still had to be taken round the land with his priestess bride.

The old ceremonies performed at our hill figures have gone. There is no fair at Uffington, no festivity at Wandlebury, no rejoicing at Tysoe or Maypole at Cerne. Nearly twenty-five years ago now, a party consisting of three members of the Society of Antiquaries and a lecturer in Anthropology made an expedition to Cerne to see if anything happened on Beltane. As youngest of the party, it fell to me to navigate the squad in the dark of the night to a concealed place in the gorse bushes above the giant's head. We approached from the north and moved for some distance under what cover was available. It is most unlikely that our approach was observed. While three of the party slept in flea-bags, one kept watch. The night passed in quiet and without incident. The only tumult which greeted Helith was the wonderful dawn chorus of the birds.

Chapter Ten

IN case I have not made things reasonably clear in the preceding pages, it seems helpful to attempt a short summary of the characteristics of these gods and goddesses. It will then be easy to see that many of them can hardly have had independent origins, but must have sprung from one idea. No invention in different localities could surely have produced such similar conceptions as Kali in India and the Cailleach and Black Annis in Britain. There is no point in labouring the matter and I shall let these short descriptions speak for themselves. No attempt has been made to rope in all the possible deities or to include all their characteristics. It would be quite easy to waste a lifetime in doing so, to the boredom and exasperation of such of Her Majesty's lieges as were confronted with the result.

The Celts of Britain always claimed that they were related to the Greeks and Trojans. A study of their gods certainly seems to show that this was true. What was the Wooden Horse of Troy but one of Magog's ceremonial figures; or Tir-nan-Og but the Gardens of the Hesperides?

At the same time there are many links with the Hindu religion, which could be expanded to much greater length than I have done here. The conclusion appears to be inescapable that all these links point to beliefs of much greater antiquity than anyone might have expected.

GREAT MOTHER OR MOON

Kali (meaning 'black') or Kali Ma (black mother). Hindu, wife of Siva. She is black with matted hair, three red eyes, one in the middle of her forehead, red palms to her hands and projecting teeth. Girdled with snakes and a necklace of human skulls, she is the goddess of death and destruction in which

160

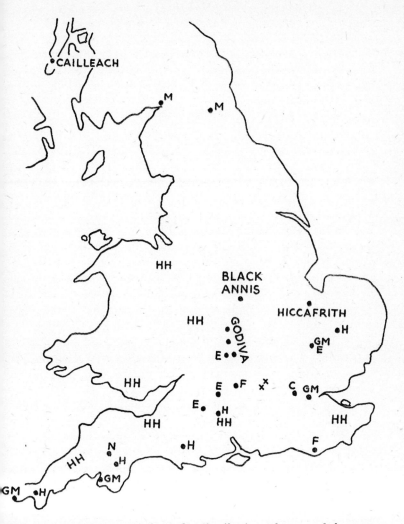

Fig. 21—Sketch-map to show the distribution of some of the more important pre-Saxon rituals in England.

E=Horse figures. GM=Gog and Magog. H=Helith. N=Nemeton. C=Cernunnos. F=Male figure, unidentified. M=Maponus. HH=Ceremonies of Hobby-horse type. × ×=Hill crosses.

Although this map only attempts to show a few of the more obvious traces of pre-Saxon religious survivals, it serves to show the improbability of any large-scale dispersal of the former population by the Anglo-Saxons.

M

capacity she carried a sacred pickaxe for digging graves. Men were sacrificed to Kali the Terrible and tortured by being hung from hooks and swung in a circle suspended from a beam. She is also, however, the goddess of fruitfulness, being identified with Maha-devi, Durga, Parvati and others. She appears to be the dark phase of the moon.

Cailleach (pronounced without sounding the 'i'. Now means old woman, witch or hag. These meanings, however, are probably derived from her nature. The name appears to come from 'caill' and to mean 'the Forest One'. Her worship covered the whole of the Highlands of Scotland, where her people were the Caledones, or Kaledonioi). She is probably identical with Yellow Muillearteach and the Gruagach; although the Gruagach may be the same goddess in a younger phase. The Cailleach has a blue-black face, one eye in the middle of her forehead and projecting teeth. The Gruagach is supposedly 'the Fair Haired One', but is also a destroyer. The Cailleach carries a hammer and thunderbolts. She is the protectress of, or is associated with, horses, deer, pigs, goats and apparently cats and snakes. She can turn herself into a standing stone.

The Cailleach kept a beautiful girl, Spring or the New Moon, imprisoned in a cave on Ben Nevis, who fled with Diarmid the Gaelic Apollo. The Cailleach controlled winds and winter. Many localities in the Highlands are associated with her and in particular her name has clung to rounded hills of breast-like shape. She is the dark phase of the moon and the Great Earth Mother. Like Kali in many particulars and even name, she was goddess both of destruction and fruitfulness. Her husband is sometimes said to have been a sea-god and perhaps Manann. Poseidon's relationship to horses should be remembered here.

Black Annis, Black Anni, or Cat Anna of Leicestershire. She had a blue face, was one-eyed and had projecting teeth. A goddess of destruction, she frequented a cave in the Dane Hills. The name of the hills may be derived from Danu, the Irish goddess, or from Diana. From the branches of an oak tree, Black Annis used to drop on the heads of passers-by and destroy them. Like the Cailleach, whom she resembles in other ways, she is therefore linked with trees and in particular with the oak, which was sacred among the Gauls of Galatia to the Goddess of Heaven. Later, with the change from the rule of women to

that of men, the oak became sacred to Zeus. Black Annis can
hardly be separated from the Cailleach. She also appears to be
Danu, or Anu.

Anu or *Danu*. Irish Mother Goddess. She is probably identical with Morrigan, who was a great slayer of men, and also
the Welsh Morgan.

Diana (apparently identical with Astarte, Ishtar, Ashtaroth,
Isis, Artemis, etc., and probably with Adraste). The Great
Earth Mother, associated with the moon, horses, deer, cattle
and fish. She had a black as well as a white phase. Although
apparently originating in Asia Minor, her cult spread over most
of the Classical World. As Ashtaroth she was the wife of Baal
the sun.

Adraste. The Goddess to whom Boadicea (Boudicca) sacrificed her female captives. The occasion was abnormal, for it
followed the violation of the sacred female royal line by
Romans. Probably the victims were normally male. Adrastea in
Classical Mythology was a nymph who suckled Zeus, but the
Egyptians held that she was put in the sky above the moon to
watch the affairs of men. Adrastea was also Nemesis and some
said Zeus was her lover. Adraste is probably Astarte and
Artemis, the full moon.

Nemon or *Nemetona*. Found in the west of England, Scotland,
Ireland and Gaul. Nemon was the Pearl of Heaven, or the moon.
Her husband Neit was an Irish god of war and slaughter. She
is probably Nemesis and Adraste. There are many place-names
connected with Nemon in Scotland and not a few in the west of
England. It seems probable that her association with sacred
groves was earlier than that of the male gods. It was perhaps to
her that white oxen were sacrificed when the mistletoe was
found growing on the oak.

Nerthus (the Danish Earth Mother). Associated with a sacred
grove on an island and thus, like the Cailleach, was goddess of
both sea and woodland. Her car was drawn by white cattle,
originally sacred to the moon. Her slaves were sacrificed by
drowning.

Epona (Gaulish horse goddess). Usually depicted as a young
woman with a horse and key of Heaven. It is probably her figure
seen riding on numerous coins of the British Iron Age, together
with a crescent moon symbol. She should be compared with the

young girl imprisoned by the Cailleach in the cave on Ben Nevis, who escaped and rode away with Diarmid, the young phase of the Gaelic Sun God. Epona's mother was a mare and father a god in human form, sometimes said to have been a mortal. She is clearly the same as Hippa of Greek mythology, who had a similar parentage. Epona represents the Earth Mother in her young phase as the new moon. Not a few English place-names probably retain her name rather than that of some imaginary Saxon.

Magog. Magg, Meg, Matrona, Maha-devi, etc. The Earth Mother and Moon Goddess in her old phase, but perhaps in all three phases. At the May Day festival she was apparently assisted by the ritual performance of the sacred marriage, which seems to take its name from her. She was also, however, the Goddess of Mayiola, the dead land, which suggests that she is the same as the Cailleach. Certainly closely connected with the horse, a symbol of fertility, she also had the cuckoo as a sacred bird. Unless the 'old woman' chose to release the cuckoos, the messengers of spring, there would be no May festival, no mays and no cuckolds. At Wandlebury she is depicted with a tired horse and waning moon, while her husband, or son, Gog, is rising to succeed her. Magog must normally be regarded as 'the old woman' of folk-lore. Like the Cailleach, her name survives on rounded hills in England. Like the Cailleach also, she is sometimes represented as a standing stone. Legends of Magog and Gog, so Mr. D. J. Prystosh tells me, are found as far east as Galicia, to the north of the Carpathian Mountains.

Godiva. Apparently the Earth Mother and Moon Goddess in her old and new phases. At first she appears on her white horse as a veiled, or blackened woman, but later at Banbury as a 'fine' lady (some versions say 'old'). There seems little doubt that she is the same as the Cailleach. There is no mention of her husband, unless he is the giant who appeared with a dragon (Celtic horse) at Burford in an Oxfordshire procession. The giant, however, was probably the demon of darkness, Wandil.

Black Demeter of Greece had a horse or pig's head with snakes in her hair. She, like the Cailleach and Black Annis was a cave-dweller and represented winter and the dark phase of the moon. Orgies of destruction and murder were performed in her name. Apparently identical with Nemesis and Adrastea.

164

Brigid, Bride, etc. Goddess of the great tribe of Brigantes who occupied most of northern England. Brigid is both old and young and some appear to equate her with Morrigan. Nevertheless, her attributes are distinct. She may perhaps be an older form of Baal, a female sun and promoter of fertility. Like Apollo she has the lifegiving apple. The war caused by Queen Cartimandua of the Brigantes, which led to the Roman conquest of northern Britain, turned on the question of who was to be the Queen's lover and may indicate that the change from matriarchy to patriarchy was still incomplete among this people. Chiefly a goddess of fire, it does not seem probable that Brigid belongs to the same group as those already mentioned, in which the Great Mother was the moon. If Brigid was the Great Mother it was as the sun. Baal, however, was once female in the same way, and later became a male sun. Our Magog appears to carry an apple.

Danu, Black Annis, or Diana, Irish goddess whose name still clings to breast-shaped hills.

GREAT FATHER OR SUN

Baal, Balor, Bel, Belenus, Beli, etc. The sun in his most powerful form. As Balor in Ireland he burnt up people on whom his eye rested. As Baleyg he is Odin in the North; the god with the flaming eyes. In Palestine he was represented as Hercules with a club. The Cerne Hercules is Helith and presumably Helios the sun. Although originally female, Baal became the husband of Ashtaroth, Ishtar, Astarte, etc. He was thus the father of all productiveness in the same way that Astarte was the mother. Human victims were certainly burnt to Baal at Beltane (1st of May), Samhain (Hallowe'en) or Hogmanay and other festivals. Baal or Bel is clearly a phase of Ogmius, Ogma Sunface, Og or Gog, who is commemorated at Hogmanay. He is also Hog of Hogmagog and the husband of Magog. In his capacity for burning people up and general destruction of human life, he is the equivalent of Siva, whose consort Kali, or Mahadevi, is the counterpart of Magog and the Cailleach. Both pairs, Bel and the Cailleach and Siva and Kali, are similarly deities of fruitfulness.

Manann. Gaelic sea-god and probably husband of the Cailleach. The Cailleach certainly had control of the sea by means of the winds and so Manann is probably the same as Bel, but perhaps in a different phase. Whether he was the same as Shony it is not possible at present to say. Manann has apparently given his name to Clackmannan, where a 'Locus Manavi' seems to be located in the Ravenna Cosmography. Since some ritual dance was performed until recently on the summit of Dumyat near Stirling, it is perhaps permissible to think that Mannan's stone, which gave its name to Clackmannan, stood there. Another locus in the Cosmography, that of 'Manopi', has been located at Clochmabenstane (a prehistoric stone circle) at Gretna in Dumfries. Mabon or Maponus was the son of Matrona. He was equated with Apollo and so it is not surprising that the tradition of runaway marriage should have survived at Gretna.

Mabon (see above). The sun in his youth, or rising phase. In this stage he is the son of Matrona, or Magog, the equivalent of Diarmid, the son of the Cailleach, and of Apollo, who was a sun god in the Classical World. The names Manann and Mabon both appear to imply relationship with Magog. This was probably once a family group. I am well aware that the root 'Ma' means 'great' in many languages, but it is also more frequently the first noise made by sheep and human beings to greet their mother. 'Great' and 'mother' were once synonymous. Diarmid ran off with the girl imprisoned by the Cailleach, who I assume to be spring and the new moon. The difficulty with all these ancient British deities lies in the impossibility of seeing them in the same light as those of the Classical World. Mabon was called Apollo by the Romans and was thus the sun and also the killer of the power of darkness, Python. But he was not necessarily the same phase as Gog, who was apparently the sun, Helios, Baal and Hercules. Jupiter and Zeus were synonymous in the Classical World, but a Celtic deity, Taranis, carries both Zeus' thunderbolt and the sun's wheel symbol. The Celtic gods are much closer to those of Asia than to the real Classical deities, although they have picked up some of the attributes of the latter.

Helith depicted as Hercules. Apparently identical with Baal, Belenus, Ogmius, etc. Associated with large stones.

Gog, Og, Hog, etc. Perhaps originally a bodiless deity corresponding to Brahma and the force at the back of all things. Later seems to have become identified with the sun and either the husband or son of Magog. Found both in the west and in Asia. Ogmius is shown on Gaulish carvings as drawing men after him by chains from his mouth to their chins. Ezekiel threatened to reverse this process with Gog. The Gauls said that it indicated the power of speech.

Cernunnos. Antler-headed god of fruitfulness. Perhaps equated both with Apollo and Mercury. Amongst other attributes he has Apollo's mouse or rat. It will be remembered that gold mice were part of the Hebrew tribute to the Philistines and presumably an offering to Baal. Cernunnos may therefore be simply another version of Baal and as much a member of this group as any of the others. He survived until Tudor times as Herne the Hunter in the Thames Valley. There are many surviving representations of Cernunnos in Gaul. It is possible to wonder whether he is not Robin Hood, who has been shown by Lord Raglan and others to be a Celtic god. If so, since Robin Hood forms a prominent feature of Helith's festival at Helston in Cornwall, his Maid Marion would then become Magog. Her name suggests that this is so. Thus we come back again to the woodlands as with Black Annis, Nemon and the Cailleach. Like Helith, Robin Hood was associated with large stones.

On the Celtic silver bowl found at Gundestrup in Jutland, Cernunnos is shown (Fig. 20b) holding a torque, a lunar symbol, in one hand and apparently strangling Python with the other. A deer looks over his shoulder. Other animals, a pig, horned domestic beasts, a dolphin and various savage species are included in the picture. Here Cernunnos has some of the attributes of both Apollo and Artemis and probably represents a stage in the change in importance from female to male rulers. No doubt this process took a long time. Apollo and Artemis in the Classical World were regarded as brother and sister and had similar attributes. The evidence here is all slight, but further information might strengthen it. Cernunnos may be 'the Man in the Moon'. It is interesting to see that on the Hebridean pottery of the Celtic Iron Age, it is the stag and lunar symbols which are most in evidence. Whether they belong to the Cailleach, her brother or perhaps her husband, we can only guess. Further discoveries might easily be made here.

Taranis. A great sky god in western Europe, perhaps the equivalent of Brahma in the East. One of a trinity with Teutates and Esus. Equated with Jupiter by the Romans. Apparently associated with bulls, serpents and wheels and so with the sun.

Teutates and *Esus*. Gaulish gods each apparently equated with both Mercury and Mars. Esus may well be the Gaulish equivalent of Zeus and was certainly associated with trees. Human victims were sacrificed to Teutates by being plunged into tubs of water. The process is shown on the Gundestrup bowl (Fig. 20*b*). This recalls the ceremonial drowning of Nerthus' slaves. Teutates may be a male Nerthus. It might be possible to show that after a passage of several hundred years Teutates became Thor and Taranis Odin. In Norse mythology, however, which appears in any case to be a mixture of at least two religious beliefs, Tyr is the son of Odin. To us, looking at it from a British angle, it may be thought that Taranis is Tyr Annis and either the son or husband of Black Annis. If so, since it seems that Black Annis is the same as the Cailleach with her thunderbolts and hammer, Taranis should be her male supplanter or husband and the equivalent of the Norse Thor.

Hiccafrith, Hiccafric or Hiccathrift. Now essentially a god of the 'marshland' country round the Wash, but apparently not unknown in western England. Armed with a wagon wheel and axle tree, he fought with a giant. He therefore has the attributes of Taranis, Jupiter and Zeus. He threw missiles at churches and was associated with a stone having some kind of raised projection on a flat base, which earned it the local name of 'candlestick' or 'collar stud'. This stone appears to have stood on a round barrow (Hiccafrith's grave), surrounded with an earthen ring. Hiccafrith's wash-basin still remains as a hollow near Smeeth station, beside a cross roads in what was formerly a wide extent of common grazing land. The barrow has been destroyed recently. It seems probable that Hiccafrith's ceremonial combat with the giant formerly took place when the cattle and horses of the rich Icenean settlements in east Norfolk were moved across the small stream, which later became the mouth of the Ouse, into the Marshland summer grazings. Hiccafirth's original name has clearly been lost and his present one seems to be an Anglo-Saxon explanation, 'Oh, he is the god the Hiccas (Iceni) trust in.'

Although the description of Hiccafrith's collar stud sounds remarkably like a Hindu 'yoni-lingam' symbol, it may be no

more than the base of a medieval wayside cross. Like Robin
Hood, Hiccafrith appears to have humanized in the Middle Ages
into a man who fought a Dane, but this did not prevent him
projecting a missile four miles from Smeeth through the wall of
Walpole St. Peter's church, where a small hole is still shown.
Judging by the place-names, the country of the Hiccas at one
time extended from Suffolk at least as far north-eastward as
Boston in Lincolnshire and south-westward to the borders of
Essex. Before the Belgic invasion the area was presumably
much greater. Hiccafrith was therefore a great god and probably
the same as Helith.

Notes

RELATIONSHIP BETWEEN THE FIGURES
AND THE TRACKWAY

Although the filling of the hollow trackway is apparently the same as that of the hollows of the figures, it has been possible to show that the track is later. The track certainly passes over part of the feet of the horse and of the goddess. There is therefore no apparent connection between these two old features of the hillside. How old the track may be, cannot at present be estimated. It may be the road along which Cole was driven from Babraham to Cambridge in 1724; or it may be an Iron Age track, which had encroached on the figures.

It is reasonable, however, to suppose that the outlines of the goddess were already invisible when the track was formed, for nobody deliberately drives over humps and hollows if they can be avoided. This tends to confirm the supposition that the goddess had vanished before Tudor times. Which figure survived as late as the time of Cole, we have yet to discover. Attempts will also have to be made to see whether the other two figures extend below the roadway.

RITUAL AT THE GODDESS FIGURE

During the progress of the excavations, various details were observed which had not been expected:—

(1) The breast area appeared to have been deliberately dug out and in particular a semi-circular trench formed round the

171

bottom of her left breast. This area had subsequently been cleaned out, new turfs thrown into it and the whole area covered with chalk rubble.

(2) A small circular pit was found beside the horse's eye filled with red earth brought from a distance, and a hollow beside this was filled with a dark deposit. This was all covered by a layer of chalk rubble.

(3) A deep area appeared to have been deliberately dug at the peak of the goddess's hair. This, like the breast area, had been cleaned out and filled with chalk rubble.

(4) A small, elongated pit was found in the outline of the goddess at the point where her legs meet the body. This contained similar dark material to that near the horse's eye. It was rich soil, containing numerous rootlets and traces of charcoal. Although it had been somewhat disturbed by the insertion of a measuring post, it was also covered by a layer of rubble containing a Belgic or Roman potsherd. The surroundings of this pit appeared to have been much soaked by liquids. At the toe of her advanced foot another hollow was found filled with the same dark material.

(5) The explanation of these phenomena, as suggested to me by Sir Cyril Fox, is that they were libation pits into which something was poured during religious ceremonies. It is yet uncertain whether chemists will be able to identify these offerings from samples of soil. It seems probable that traces of an older ritual were removed when the larger figures were added to the hill-side. The goddess was re-dedicated in perhaps a milder form. One suspects that the offering in these libation pits was the blood of sacrifices, which promoted a strong growth of vegetation.

From these details I conclude that the goddess was at first a somewhat ferocious personality. A goddess of death and destruction, who at the same time carried an apple of life in her left hand and indicated her maternal character with her right. Later she was turned into the milder moon goddess to whom blood offerings were no longer made.

SURVIVAL OF THE WHITE HORSE CULT IN IRELAND

In Giraldus Cambrensis' *Topography of Ireland* we find a vivid picture of an ancient rite connected with the White Horse. The following translation of Chapter XXV is taken from Bohn's Edition of Giraldus:—

'There are some things which shame would prevent my relating, unless the course of my subject required it. For a filthy story seems to reflect a stain on the author, although it may display his skill. But the severity of history does not allow us either to sacrifice truth or affect modesty; and what is shameful in itself may be related by pure lips in decent words. There is, then, in the northern and most remote part of Ulster, namely, at Kenel Cunil, a nation which practises a most barbarous and abominable rite in creating their king. The whole people of that country being gathered in one place, a white mare is led into the midst of them, and he who is to be inaugurated, not as a prince but as a brute, not as a king but as an outlaw, comes before the people on all fours, confessing himself a beast with no less impudence than imprudence. The mare being immediately killed, and cut in pieces and boiled, a bath is prepared for him from the broth. Sitting in this, he eats of the flesh which is brought to him, the people standing round and partaking of it also. He is also required to drink of the broth in which he is bathed, not drawing it in any vessel, nor even in his hand, but lapping it with his mouth. These unrighteous rites being duly accomplished, his royal authority and dominion are ratified.'

Kenel Cunil is apparently Tirconnell, the present Donegal. This seems to have been part of the land of the Fir Domnan, the Dumnonii or Damnonii. In this rite the king was evidently supposed to change himself into a white mare. It seems reasonable to suppose that originally it was the matriarchal queen who underwent this ceremony, but with the change to male rule, the king was compelled to perform it.

Giraldus appears to have obtained the materials for his book in A.D. 1185

My friend, Mr. John Lorne Campbell, has also drawn my

attention to a description of a priest in this same area who ornamented his church with symbols of the sun and moon.

TENTATIVE TIME SCALE

± 200 B.C.	Construction of Iron Age fort at Wandlebury and start of Horse Goddess ritual festival by Iceni.
± 50 B.C.	Displacement of Iceni by Belgic Catuvellauni. Construction of two male giants and addition of chariot. No evidence as yet of Belgic Occupation of Wandlebury.
± A.D. 100	Goddess figure had become worn into hollows by rain washing down the outlines and probably by scraping to clean the outlines before festivities. Deep hollows were filled in on top of accumulated rain washed sludge and a layer of fresh chalk spread on top. This is very roughly dated by small fragments of Romano-British grey ware pottery beneath the fresh chalk and a minute fragment of terra-sigillata in the chalk layer itself. Other fragments of pottery are of uncertain date. A second layer of fresh chalk was subsequently applied on the breast of the goddess. Some occupation of Wandlebury in Roman times.
c. A.D. 1600	Festivities at Wandlebury by University scholars forbidden.
c. A.D. 1724	Last time a giant in known to have been seen by an antiquary.
c. A.D. 1730	Lord Godolphin walled in the interior of Wandelbury and diverted roadways.
c. A.D. 1850	Giant still visible from Sawston, to be soon concealed by planting of a belt of beech trees below the figures. Ploughing of hill-side may have originated in Napoleonic Wars.
c. A.D. 1941	Site reploughed.

VISIBILITY OF HILL FIGURES

It has been suggested to me that the Wandelbury giants could not have been hill figures because the low angle of slope, just at the summit of the hill, would prevent their being clearly seen from below. This is undoubtedly correct, but has nothing to do with the question. As Mr. Tebbutt pointed out to me, the Uffington White Horse cannot be seen properly from below and is in a precisely similar situation to those at Wandlebury. It can only be reasonably well seen from Dragon Hill, just as the Wandlebury figures could only be properly appreciated from Little Trees Hill. It is interesting too to note that the burial of a horse is associated in local tradition with the barrow on the top of Little Trees Hill. This barrow has not been excavated.

As I have said before, these hill figures are survivals from a ritual and were not intended as images to be worshipped. It did not matter whether they could be widely seen from a distance or not. It should be remembered that the views obtained of these figures by air photographs are not those of the people who designed them. The very fact that the figures are not placed where they are clearly visible from a wide area is an additional reason for regarding them as being purely ritualistic. The same is true of such things as the Serpent Mounds of America.

The reason why our remaining figures are found on slopes may be very simple. To people living on high hill-tops all level ground was valuable. If therefore some place near their homes had to be dedicated to a yearly ceremony, a site on a slope was greatly to be preferred. That too is why at Uffington and Wandlebury the figures are at the top of the slope. It was the nearest available situation.

Index